AN ORAL HISTORY OF GESTALT THERAPY

INTERVIEWS WITH LAURA PERLS
ISADORE FROM
ERVING POLSTER
MIRIAM POLSTER
ELLIOTT SHAPIRO

Joe Wysong
Edward Rosenfeld

The Gestalt Journal
Gouldsboro, Maine

for:

Paul Goodman
Frederick Perls
William Warner
Paul Weisz

in remembrance

A Publication of The Gestalt Journal Press

Published by:

The Gestalt Journal Press, Inc.
A Division of:
The Center for Gestalt Development, Inc.
P. O. Box 278
Gouldsboro ME 04607-0278
U.S.A.

ISBN: 978-0-939266-08-1

CONTENTS

INTRODUCTION

When *The Gestalt Journal* began publication plans in 1977, we decided to initiate a series of interviews with those in the Gestalt community who had been involved in the development of Gestalt therapy since its inception in the late 1940's.

Our choices were obvious and our interview with Laura Perls appeared in the premier issue of the *Journal* in 1978. Interviews with Isadore From, and Erving and Miriam Polster appeared in the next two issues. Our interview with educational innovator Elliott Shapiro, also among those involved in the germination of Gestalt therapy, appeared later.

As no publication devoted to Gestalt therapy existed before publication of *The Gestalt Journal*, we had no idea of the demand for these issues and we soon depleted our supply.

It became clear from the many requests we received that the greatest level of interest was for our series of interviews. Rather than reprinting our early issues, we decided instead to combine all four interviews in a single volume and offer them as a complete unit.

Rather than updating the introductions to each interview, we have left them as originally written. The interview with Laura Perls appeared in Volume I, No. 1 (Winter, 1978), the interview with Isadore From in Volume I, No. 2 (Fall, 1978), the interview with Erving & Miriam Polster in Volume II, No. 1 (Spring, 1979), and the interview with Elliott Shapiro in Volume VIII, No. 2 (Fall, 1985).

Our attempt was not only to provide an informal history of the theoretical influences on the development of Gestalt therapy, but also to capture some sense of the personalities intimately involved in Gestalt's beginnings.

We hope we've succeeded.

Joe Wysong
Editor, *The Gestalt Journal*
Highland, New York
Fall, 1989

AN ORAL HISTORY OF GESTALT THERAPY PART ONE: A CONVERSATION WITH LAURA PERLS

Edward Rosenfeld

This interview inaugurates what will be a continuing series in The Gestalt Journal. *In future issues we will be presenting conversations with the founders, originators and developers of Gestalt therapy.*

We begin, in this first issue, with a conversation with Dr. Laura Perls, who, with her husband, Frederick S. ("Fritz") Perls, began the development of Gestalt therapy more than thirty years ago. Laura Perls was originally trained in Gestalt psychology and as a psychoanalyst. She was one of the founders of the New York Institute for Gestalt Therapy.

I first met Laura in 1966. I went to her with a question: how can I become a Gestalt therapist? She answered my question then, and continued to provide advice and support over the years. In 1975, I joined her professional training group.

When the planning began for The Gestalt Journal *I wanted to find some way to let Gestalt therapists present, in their own words, a coherent picture of what Gestalt therapy is, how it developed and how it has grown, and who has been involved in it. This series of interviews I hope will provide such material.*

The bulk of this first interview is a verbatim transcript of a conversation I had with Laura Perls on the 23rd of May, 1977.

Edward Rosenfeld: You say there is no body work in addition to Gestalt therapy.

Laura Perls: This is something that I can't emphasize enough. Body work is part of Gestalt therapy. Gestalt therapy is a holistic therapy. This means that it takes the *total* organism into account, not just the voice, the verbal, the acting out and whatever.

ER: What do you think happens when somebody tries to "combine" the Feldenkrais approach, for example, with Gestalt therapy?

LP: The haven't understood, really, what Gestalt is. For instance, Ilana Rubenfeld is not combining, she is integrating certain approaches that she has studied for a long time. She has worked with the Alexander technique for twenty years and the Feldenkrais work is a kind of extension of that. I knew the work of Feldenkrais thirty years ago and it was nothing new to me because my body approach in Gestalt doesn't come from Wilhelm Reich or Moshe Feldenkrais or F. M. Alexander or J. L. Moreno or anyone, but it comes from modern dance which I've been doing since I was eight years old.

ER: Do you feel that the approach to the body comes from the individual therapist?

LP: Anything that is used comes from the individual therapist. It is what hopefully he has assimilated and integrated so that it has become a part of his background, something that he can rely on; and from the ongoing awareness in the therapeutic situation. Different therapists work with very different approaches. Isadore From doesn't use much of a body approach. He came from philosophy originally, so that's what he moves from or what moves him.

ER: Do you think it is a mistake when people study Reichian technique or study the other approaches to the body?

LP: I don't think it is a mistake if they can really, fully assimilate it. But to just take a workshop here and a workshop there and then say they combine it, that is just not good enough. It's not an integration.

ER: Let's talk about assimilation.

LP: This really is how Gestalt started, originally in South Africa. It started from the concept of resistance which was always understood in psychoanalysis as an anal feature. Then Fritz Perls wrote a paper, for a psychoanalytical conference held in Czechoslovakia in 1936, titled "Oral

Resistances.'' That paper was originally based on some research that I had done earlier, in Berlin, when my child was born: the methods of feeding and weaning infants.

ER: Were you already a psychologist when you were living in Berlin?

LP: I had a doctorate in psychology and I was trained in psychoanalysis; I had my analysis behind me already. I still trained at the Berlin Institute and, later, in Amsterdam. I was first a Gestaltist and then became an analyst. Fritz was an analyst first and then came to Gestalt and never quite got into it.

ER: Was the Gestalt psychological approach then basically perceptual? Were you interested in working experimentally?

LP: It was expanded through the work of Kurt Goldstein into a whole organismic approach. Fritz had worked with Goldstein and so had I. Fritz was an assistant of his for a few months and I was his student for a number of years. I did a lot of experimental work at the Institute for Brain-Injured Veterans.

ER: Let's go back to the research that you were doing that led to Fritz' paper on oral resistances.

LP: I was mainly interested in the methods of feeding and weaning because my experiences right from the hospital and what I had read about the feeding of children were very unsatisfactory to me. The way things are stuffed into little kids. The feeding is . . . it leads to introjection. They are not allowed enough time to chew.

ER: What about infants, breast-feeding and weaning?

LP: Weaning is often done very early or very late; and the foods that children get first are completely mashed and meally. Mothers are very impatient. Children drink the food instead of learning to chew. Chewing takes time and patience and an awareness of what one is chewing. I pay a lot of attention to the way people eat. I concentrate on the detailed activities of doing something: chewing as well as studying, putting on one's clothing, having a bath or walking in the street. Minute work.

ER: Do you see a connection between assimilation and patience?

LP: Between assimilation and taking time. Drinking doesn't take any time. You swallow immediately without any intermediate process. The eating process is an awares process.

ER: In essence the beginning of Gestalt therapy comes in terms of eating: it

grew up around the whole concept of how we eat.
LP: How we eat, get hold of something and make it assimilable.
ER: The way in which we focus on it, break it down, deal with the different parts.
LP: The taste of it, the texture of it, the way it goes. When you swallow the unchewed it lies heavy in your stomach. Either you feel like repeating it or it passes through in an undigested way.
ER: How did this differ from what were then, the current psychoanalytic theories?
LP: Psychoanalytic theory, I think, identifies assimilation and introjection.
ER: Were the psychoanalysts discussing all the resistances, in addition to the anal ones?
LP: I think Freud said that development takes place through introjections, but if it remains introjection and goes no further, then it becomes a block; it becomes identification. Introjection is to a great extent unawares. And actually what we see with every patient is that they imitate consciously, and with awareness, what they admire and what they like, but they introject, unawares, what they can't stomach in any other way.
ER: But yet they feel they need, even if unawares. . .
LP: They don't even feel that with awareness, they don't really feel it. But what it does is that it avoids the external conflict and leads to the identification with the disagreeable features of father or mother or whoever teaches. It avoids the external conflict but sets up an internal one which becomes a block.
ER: What I don't understand is what was so radical about Fritz' new theory of resistances. I've been re-reading *Ego, Hunger and Aggression,* and. . .
LP: What do you find radical?
ER: It's not so radical for me because I don't come out of the Freudian background. In addition to reading *Ego, Hunger and Aggression* I've been re-reading *In and Out the Garbage Pail* and trying to get some sense of how Gestalt therapy developed. What I keep seeing is that the basic background is Freudian psychoanalysis; in addition to Gestalt psychology, but psychoanalysis was the pervasive psychological *weltanschuanng*.
LP: Actually in the beginning, when *Ego, Hunger and Aggression* was written, we still called ourselves psychoanalysts, but revisionists.
ER: Right. *Ego, Hunger and Aggression* was subtitled: "A Revision of

Freud's Theory and Method.'' But what I don't understand as being so radical is the paper: ''Oral Resistances'' and the material about the assimilation of the introject and so forth. Was all this so foreign to the Freudian ear of those times?

LP: Yes. It flew in the face of their resistance theory: anal development. We also rejected the libido theory.

ER: The message I got from Fritz' recounting of those times was that he went to the 1936 Czech conference feeling that whatever he had worked out was a contribution to psychoanalysis and that he would become a greater psychoanalyst.

LP: He was pretty much rejected there, apart from one or two people. One was my former analyst who we were friendly with. His name was Karl Landauer and he was killed by the Nazis, that's why nobody knows him. He started the Frankfurt Psychoanalytic Institute with Frieda Fromm-Reichman and Heinrich Meng. They were my first teachers. Landauer was my analyst and Frieda was my first teacher in psychoanalysis.

ER: You went through a thorough analysis as part of your training?

LP: Two and one-half years, every day.

ER: And at the same time you were working with the Gestalt psychologists? You were working with Goldstein?

LP: At the same time. It was very contradictory and I got awfully confused to the extent that I nearly went to sleep, like Pavlov's double-conditioned dogs.

ER: It was too much.

LP: Yes. Somehow it didn't go together. They went against each other to quite an extent; and it takes a lifetime to integrate.

ER: Were you still working with Landauer when you went to Amsterdam?

LP: No. I had finished my analysis in 1928 or 1929 and I got married in 1930. Landauer was our friend, later, in Amsterdam.

ER: Did you have a practice when you went to South Africa?

LP: In Berlin I had just started my practice; I had a few patients. I was still under supervision with Otto Feinichel. He was a great writer and theorist but a lousy teacher! He didn't say anything at all. It was wasted time and wasted money. He just sat there and listened to my report and apparently agreed with most of it; and he said nothing.

ER: When you went to South Africa, I know Fritz started a practice . . .

LP: I started after three months because I didn't speak English.
ER: And Fritz did?
LP: Fritz had been in America already. Inflation you know, 1923-1924, inflation caused him to leave Germany and he went to America. He thought he would stay but he didn't like it then. It was just too crude for him at that point. He came from Berlin which was at that time really the European center of cultural development: everything, Max Reinhardt, Brecht, Kurt Weil, the Bauhous, great writers.
ER: Once you had started to learn some English you started your practice in South Africa; whose idea was it to set up a psychoanalytic institute? Was that decided before you went there?
LP: That is really the purpose that we went there for. We were sent out by the International Association; by Ernest Jones who was the president at that time. He got us to South Africa, he was the man who had applied for someone to go there. He was at first very friendly and very helpful. But then he went to the Lucerne conference in 1938, and a stink was made and it was decided that nobody who was not already in Europe, as a trainer, could be a trainer or teacher anywhere else. So we had to give up our training institute in South Africa. But by that point we had such an established practice there. It was during the war. I worked ten to thirteen hours a day, six days a week and sometimes on Sunday. I was in my thirties and early forties and I was very energetic then. Once I came into the kitchen, by 8 o'clock at night and said to the maid: "I am completely pooped." She answered: "What do you do? You sit and talk!"
By then already, in the late 1930's, I paid a lot of attention not only to what people said and to interpretation, but to their breathing and their co-ordination. I started doing body work and sitting opposite my patients. At that time Fritz was still addicted to the couch and never quite got rid of it. But I never used it again. If I wanted someone to lie down I had them lie on the floor because that was much more even support and we could do certain experiments with co-ordination and alignment.
ER: What was the reaction of your patients when you sat face to face with them? Weren't they coming into therapy expecting a typical psychoanalyst?
LP: They didn't know anything.
ER: They didn't? So it was more of a naive group.

LP: Much more. And there were others that were very interested and they welcomed it. Actually, while I was sitting behind the patient I knitted; because otherwise I would have had to smoke cigarettes, like Fritz did. I smoked very little, not even a half a pack a day and I gave it up, already, some fifteen years ago. But Fritz smoked two, three, four packs a day.

ER: I remember: the hand and the cigarette.

LP: I think he could have lived ten years longer if he hadn't smoked.

ER: There's a section in *Garbage Pail* where he says something like: "What I really should be writing about is my problem with smoking; that's my real problem."

LP: It's a problem of settling aggressive energy; muscular energy, that's what nicotine does.

ER: It settles the aggressive energy?

LP: It interferes with the muscle tone; it reduces the muscle tone. One smokes a peace pipe.

ER: When Fritz returned from the rejection of the 1936 Czech conference, did you then start working more actively together trying to evolve a new therapy, or was it more gradual?

LP: We continued discussing things. Then Fritz went into the army, from 1942 to 1946 and he had time to write. He came home mostly every weekend and later at least once or twice a month. He started to put things together. But we had a friend who helped us a lot with the English. Fritz' English, in spite of getting started earlier, was pretty atrocious. My pronunciation was always worse, his was better. The north Germans can speak English better than the south Germans.

ER: Where in south Germany are you from?

LP: I am from Baden. We speak French better, our pronunciation in French is better.

ER: So someone helped Fritz with the English . . .

LP: We had a friend who helped with the writing. He was a writer, an historian and a very bright guy, a friend of ours.

ER: Do you remember his name?

LP: He was a Dutchman. His name was Hugo Postumys. The name he was known under was Jumbo.

ER: What made you leave South Africa?

LP: Several reasons. Partly political. Because Jan Smuts (then Prime

Minister of South Africa, author of *Holism and Evolution*) was retiring and a young man of about forty-three, a very brilliant guy, a *wunderkind*, who was supposed to succeed him, suddenly died of a heart attack and there was no one who was in the Union party, which was the democratic party, to have a chance to be elected. We knew what would be coming because the nationalists had been working all along. They were pretty well organized and we wanted to leave before the 1948 elections. Fritz left in 1946 and I left in 1947.

ER: Were there friends here who drew you to New York City?

LP: No. No. Nothing. We had already applied for immigration before we went to South Africa but the quota for the U.S. was filled and we couldn't get in. We had an affidavit from Dr. Brill who was the president of the American Psychoanalytic Association.

ER: And that enabled you to enter this country?

LP: No. Later on we got another affidavit from Karen Horney, whom Fritz worked with for a short time before she came to America. He worked with her first and then with Wilhelm Reich.

ER: He mentions her advice in one of his books: "The only one who could help you is Wilhelm Reich."

LP: Yes. Yes!

ER: So it was through Karen Horney that you came to America?

LP: My brother was here already and he guaranteed for us, but he had just started his own business. My brother started here with ten marks in his pocket as a Fuller brush man, going from door-to-door. Now he has made it again.

ER: Were you already in America when *Ego, Hunger and Aggression* was published?

LP: No. It was published first in South Africa, before it was published in England. Then for a long time it was not published here, not until Fritz was out at Esalen when it was published by Orbit Graphic Press. Then it was re-published by Random House.

ER: So it came out first in South Africa and that was while you were still living there?

LP: Yes.

ER: What were the reactions to those ideas in South Africa?

LP: The people who understood anything about it at all were the people that we had been working with. They did write-ups in the newspapers that were very favorable and the book was taken up quite eagerly by Allen & Unwin in England. But it didn't go well in England and they didn't re-publish later.

ER: Did you train people in South Africa? Did Fritz?

LP: We started to train people but then we weren't allowed to anymore because of the decision, by the psychoanalytic association (which we were still members of), to restrict training to those who were already trainers in Europe.

ER: Were you calling it concentration therapy then?

LP: Then we were still calling it psychoanalysis. Even when we came to New York; I found some old stationery where we had both of our names on it as psychoanalysts. We changed it really with the publication of the book *Gestalt Therapy*, in 1950.

ER: You came to America and settled on the upper West Side of New York City.

LP: Fritz was here already a year before. And he was, for six months, in Canada before he could get his permanent residence visa. He visited my brother; they invited him and he stayed with them for three weeks, which was a disaster. They advised him not to settle in New York because there was too much competition. They had no idea of our professional potential.

ER: I suppose the fear was that you would be lost in the crowd of all the analysts in New York.

LP: So he started in New Haven and that was about the worst thing he could have done. At that time the chair for psychiatry was vacant at Yale and everybody thought that he was after it. So there was a kind of concerted front against him.

ER: Did he get involved in academic politics?

LP: Well he didn't get involved because he . . .

ER: They cut him out?

LP: You know Fritz either had to be accepted or he was devasted. He was just at the point of coming back to South Africa when he visited New York for a few days and spoke to Erich Fromm. Fromm said: "I don't know why you don't come here. I guarantee you that in three months you'll have a practice." In three weeks he had a practice.

ER: So he had a practice by the time you came over.

LP: He had a practice and was very busy already. I brought the children and started working immediately because Fritz couldn't accept anyone anymore. We got patients through the William Alanson White Institute at that time. Fritz got friendly with Clara Thompson and she sent a lot of people. The White Institute wanted him as a training analyst, but they wanted him to go back to medical school and get his medical degree here in the States because his European degree was not valid here. But Fritz was in his early fifties already and he didn't want to go to school anymore. At that point, when one goes to school, one goes as a teacher, not as a student. And it wasn't really necessary. Then we made contact with Paul Goodman, who had a very Reichian orientation at that time: he was in a Reichian analysis. And we made contact with lots of others, people like Dwight McDonald and other writers and artists.

ER: Who do you remember from that circle? Was Erich Fromm one of the people you continued to be in contact with?

LP: No. No, we got patients, actually trainees, from the White Institute, people whose training therapy they couldn't complete. I remember particularly two with whom I worked who later were accepted as members of the White Institute. One is someone who died last year, who headed a school for schizophrenic children who at that time was a teacher at Kings County and Elliott Shapiro was his principal. A whole line of people came to us through Elliott. Elliott gave the first training in Gestalt therapy for educators.

ER: How did Paul Weiss become involved?

LP: That was, I think, through his wife, who was a psychiatrist at Bellevue and was working with Fritz. He became a patient of Fritz' and then later worked mostly with me. Then whole chains of people came from Bellevue and from Kings County, from the Veterans Administration Hospital and from Columbia. Richard Kitzler came from Columbia; he was the psychologist for the Columbia psychiatrist who worked with Fritz, too. That was Dr. Montague who died early.

ER: Where did Isadore From come in?

LP: Isadore came as a patient and I worked with him for a number of years.

ER: Did you have contact with any of the Gestalt psychology people who were at the New School?

LP: They rejected us completely . . .

ER: Was this after the publication of *Gestalt Therapy* or beforehand?

LP: Before we didn't know them and afterwards they rejected us.
ER: Just because you use the word "Gestalt"?
LP: They felt that "Gestalt" was their domain and that it was mainly confined to perceptual psychology, which I had worked with a lot in the past. My doctorate was in visual perception.
ER: When you came to America and Fritz was already here, were you both working with the idea that you were developing something new? Was that in the air?
LP: That was in the air because *Ego, Hunger and Aggression* had been published already and some people got interested in it. Then *Gestalt Therapy* was published. When we started the New York Institute for Gestalt Therapy forty people appeared for our first course given in America.
ER: How did that book, *Gestalt Therapy*, come about?
LP: First there was a manuscript that Fritz had already written, he had been working on it. I had been working on it, too, but at that point I was satisfied to leave the glory to him. In *Ego, Hunger and Aggression* there are at least two chapters which I wrote completely: the chapters on the dummy complex and the one on insomnia. He gave me credit in the first introduction to *Ego, Hunger and Aggression*, but that credit was removed when Random House republished it. A friend wrote to Random House requesting that they re-insert the original introduction in any new edition, but they refused.
ER: That credit is still in the introduction in the Orbit Graphic Press edition of *Ego, Hunger and Aggression*. So Fritz had a manuscript, that you both had been working on, which extended the ideas about introjection, projection, retroflection and confluence.
LP: Yes. Mainly the existential orientation. Actually when we first started we wanted to call it "Existential therapy," but then existentialism was so much indentified with Sartre, with the nihilistic approach, that we looked for another name. I thought that with Gestalt therapy, with the word "Gestalt," we could get into difficulties. But that criticism was rejected by Fritz and Paul.
ER: Paul Goodman?
LP: Yes. Paul was originally hired as an editor, but then he contributed so much, particularly to the second part, which without him would never have become a coherent theory, that Paul became a co-author.
ER: Was Richard Kitzler responsible for the connection to Ralph Hefferline

at Columbia?
LP: No.
ER: How did Hefferline come into the picture?
LP: He came as a client.
ER: Did he want to do the experiments with the students at Columbia?
LP: He was interested. . . and he did the experiments at Columbia and then became a co-author with Fritz and Paul. But he never really became a member of the New York Institute for Gestalt Therapy. He did one or two seperate lectures by invitation but he did not become a part of the on-going teaching and training process.
ER: Was the Institute already established when the work started on what was to become the book, *Gestalt Therapy?*
LP: No. No, the Institute was started as a result of the publication of *Gestalt Therapy*. In 1952 the Institute started and in 1953 the Cleveland Institute for Gestalt Therapy started. We gave a ten-day intensive course at the end of 1952 or early 1953, and people from outside the city came and three people from Cleveland attended. They then started a Gestalt group there and Fritz and Paul Weiss and I and Paul Goodman went to Cleveland, more or less regularly. Then Isadore From went there for six or seven years, once or twice a month for four days at a time and trained everybody, individually and in group.
ER: Was Arthur Ceppos (of Julian Press, the original publisher of *Gestalt Therapy*) a patient?
LP: No, he was not a patient. He came to a group for a while. His then girl friend was a therapist and she came into group and into therapy.
ER: How did he become interested in the project?
LP: He was always after new things. I don't know how that started. Those negotiations were between Fritz and Art Ceppos.
ER: I've heard that what is now part two, the theoretical part, was originally supposed to be the first part.
LP: Ceppos counteradvised because at that time the "how-to" books were in vogue. He felt it would help the sale of the book if we changed it around. But for anyone who is a serious student of Gestalt therapy, the second part is really a theoretical and methodological introduction, while the other part is really experiments and practical work.
ER: Fritz mentions in *Garbage Pail* that he discussed ideas with Paul Weiss.

LP: Paul Weiss had a brilliant mind and was highly educated and very critical. Fritz liked to talk to him on occasion, but ongoingly he wouldn't have been able to cope with him. Fritz never could cope with peers for a long time. Actually we started drifting apart when I became a peer in experience and got a growing reputation as a therapist. I stuck it out in New York. Fritz could never have stayed in New York. There was too much competition and criticism and Fritz felt devastated by the slightest criticism. Paul Weiss was very critical.

ER: Were you both, you and Fritz, interested in existential philosophy before?

LP: Oh, certainly. It was part of my academic education. I worked for many years with Paul Tillich. As a student I read Kierkegaard and Heidegger; also the phenomenologists: Husserl and Scheler.

ER: What happened once *Gestalt Therapy* was published? Was it well received?

LP: It had a mixed reception. Actually Arthur Ceppos said at that time that the book would go very slowly in the beginning and in ten years would become a classic and he was right.

ER: Then what happened in the development of Gestalt therapy? Did you stay here in New York with the "peers"? With Paul Weiss, Paul Goodman and Isadore From?

LP: Actually, that was my first therapy group: It was Paul Weiss, Paul Goodman, Elliott Shapiro and two artists. It was the first group I ever worked with. I was scared at first. I had never taught before and I had never worked with groups. I was a private person always. I have been going much more public, since then, but still a lot of time for and by myself.

ER: Do you think that Gestalt therapy has changed much since those days in the early 1950's?

LP: The change is with everybody who practices it. Gestalt therapy has penetrated into all kinds of other set-ups. It has certainly become part of the program at professional schools everywhere. On the West coast it is probably the dominant therapy. Here, on the East coast, it is probably on a par with behaviorism, which is the other approach that is in the forefront.

ER: Has anything happened to Gestalt therapy in terms of theory, the methodological background, since that very exciting period a quarter of a century ago?

LP: Gesalt therapy was conceived as a comprehensive, organismic approach. But later on, particularly in the West, but in the East, too, it became identified mostly with what Fritz did at the time. It became very well-known in the last five years of his life when he was predominantly using his hot-seat method. That method is fine for demonstration workshops, but you can't carry on a whole therapy that way; yet people do. I think they are limiting themselves and doing a lot of harm.

ER: What do you think made Fritz say that individual therapy was obsolete?

LP: Because it was obsolete for him. He couldn't be bothered anymore. But don't forget that the people that he worked with in his last years were only professional people, most of whom had their own therapies already and were already active in the profession. You can work differently with those groups than you can work with a patient group, particularly with very sick patients. Until three years ago I worked with a lot of patients, not just training. But now I do only training. It's getting too much. I've done individual therapy and group therapy for forty years plus and that's enough. There's not enough coming back from the work with the patients for me.

ER: Is training more fulfilling?

LP: It's more interesting with different people and with very accomplished people. I work a lot in Europe and that is different than working with professionals here.

ER: You've been on sabatical for the past year. What have you been doing?

LP: Very little that can be talked about. I did a lot of things for myself. A lot of reading, lots of music.

ER: What have you been reading that's been interesting? What's been turning you on?

LP: I've been re-reading Nietzsche; and I've been reading *whole* books again, as opposed to just dipping in and reading magazines, professional and otherwise. I've read in the last fifteen years mainly literary magazines, like *The New York Review of Books*. But now I'm reading the literature and a lot of new poetry.

I've been going through things that I've written over the years, published and unpublished, mostly unpublished, and trying to make something of it. But it's more in my head, still, than it is on paper.

ER: Would you like to produce a book out of all these materials?

LP: That's what I'm asked to do. If I produce anything it will be two books:

one a collection of articles, published ones and unpublished ones, and I may write one or two more that I am interested in at the moment. I'm mostly asked for a kind of autobiography, but I can't write a straight-forward autobiography, just the facts, it bores me.
ER: Do you have another approach?
LP: I've had an approach for many years already. I started in the 1940's writing stories; they were mostly taken off from relevant experiences in my youth and life.
ER: Are you writing more stories or going back to the ones you've already written?
LP: I'm going through them again and, of course, they have to be connected in some way so that it will end up being a blend of truth and fiction. A myth is always truer than the facts: it's an integration of experiences.
ER: How do you see Gestalt therapy today?
LP: Oh, it is in many ways blossoming. In many ways I have a lot of reservations because what's been done with it is the same thing that has been done with psychoanalysis and other approaches which have become more well known and popular. It has become simplified and falsified and distorted and misrepresented. A lot of the work that I'm doing now, where ever I give a workshop or work with people in Gestalt, is really to emphasize that and confront them with what I think is important.
ER: For instance. . .
LP: Important is the ongoing Gestalt formation. And to take the patient, or whoever you are working with, where they are—not imposing on them certain methods; that is an encounter therapy. Gestalt therapy, in the true sense, is not an encounter therapy.
ER: But it is moment to moment.
LP: It is moment to moment and acknowledges whatever comes up from the past as a memory which you are having now and therefore must have some significance now. Then we can interpolate between the past and what is now.
ER: But doesn't encounter, from its roots in T-groups onward, lean very heavily on Gestalt and some of the other existential psychotherapies in terms of the present tense orientation. . . . And yet you're saying. . .
LP: Yes, but to a very great extent they have a very fixed method of confronting which I think is a mistake and if it's applied in Gestalt then it's not

really Gestalt.

ER: But there is a methodology in Gestalt therapy. Isn't there an informing background that as a Gestalt therapist I'm always using?

LP: As a Gestalt therapist: Gestalt therapy is existential, experiential and experimental. But what techniques you use to implement that and to apply it, that depends to the greatest extent on your background, on your experiences professionally, in life, your skills and whatever. The Gestalt therapist uses himself and herself with whatever they have got and whatever seems to apply, at the time, to the actual situation: a patient, a group, a trainee, whatever.

ER: I've been in training with you and with Isadore From and the things that have come up for me, what I call the informing background of the therapeutic work I do, are methodological and theoretical concerns: like the contact boundary, the how of contact.

LP: Experience is on the boundary. Within the boundaries there is to a great extent unawareness and confluence. If you go too quickly beyond the boundary you may feel unsupported, actually, that's what I work with: a concept and experience of contact *and* support. Certain supports are necessary and essential. Other supports are, well, desirable and possibly usable. The lack of essential support always results in anxiety. That is actually what anxiety is.

ER: A lack of essential supports . . .

LP: Trying to make contact for which the essential support is lacking. You see, usually anxiety is interpreted as lack of oxygen. But that is a secondary thing already. It's just one of the supports that may be missing; or that even is actually mobilized when an essential support is missing; in order to withdraw and play possum. An infant, for instance, feels anxious when it is not held secure. You may feel great anxiety when you are hungry and your body isn't functioning properly.

ER: What about concepts like confluence, projection, introjection and retroflection; for example, when I see a client biting his lip. These are the concepts that I see missing in encounter-oriented or demonstration style Gestalt therapy.

LP: They do not go into the details of when and how a person is unable to live on the boundary. Without a clear boundary experience the person is open to introjection and projection.

ER: So the projection and introjection grow out of a lack of what you are calling the essential supports. Through the development of anxiety we then try to gobble up something whole or screen it away from us, project it on to someone or something else.
LP: Well, introjection always occurs when you are confronted too quickly with something that you can't cope with and assimilate. Either you reject it and withdraw from it or you introject it. What happens mostly in schools is a lot of stuff is presented in a way in which it is expected to be repeated on the exam. People swallow it whole and spew it out on the exam and are rid of it forever after. I've never seen people who after having learned so much and stayed in school for so many years know so very little as here in this country; it's ghastly.
ER: Do you think as an intellectual viewpoint, as a way of looking at the world and looking at what goes on in the world of ideas, that Gestalt is a valid, descriptive metaphor: an analogue for what happens.
LP: Gestalt is an aesthetic concept. Mainly Gestalt is an aesthetic concept, but Kohler used it in connection with field theory which originally is an idea from physics, a physical theory. Kohler was, I think, originally a physicist.
ER: Yes. He studied field theory with Max Planck before he did the Gestalt psychology work with Max Wertheimer and Kurt Koffka.
LP: That Greek word for awareness, aisthanomai, "I am aware," the root for aesthetics, that word is a medium form between active and passive.
ER: In the mystical sense, like the space between breathing in and breathing out. The awareness.
LP: Goldstein, in *The Organism*, and much earlier, maintains that sensing is an active process; it's not just receiving the impression.
ER: Isn't that the whole point of Gestalt formation?
LP: Exactly, certainly . . .
ER: We do make choices, whether awares or unawares. We make a choice in terms of . . .
LP: Interest . . .
ER: . . . of what is dominant for us.
LP: What becomes figure is what is of greatest interest for the organism at the time. And then, of course, always, how the figure relates to its background. Because that is what gives it meaning. If it doesn't relate then we say it's meaningless. it's senseless, it's bizarre. But sometimes it's the

lack of background in the therapist that causes that, when he calls something bizarre or meaningless that is very meaningful to the patient. It is desireable that the therapist have more awareness and experience than the patient and more knowledge. If you have a very well educated, erudite patient and you know nothing, or almost nothing, beyond your professional stuff, you can't cope.

ER: Have you had experiences like that?

LP: Very little. I've learned from my patients. But I have a very wide background, compared with many of the people here I have probably a wider and deeper educational background than most of them.

ER: The dance and the music. . .

LP: An all-around education. I went to a humanistic *gymnasium*; I had nine years of Latin and six of Greek. I can still read Greek.

ER: We don't do that anymore; we don't have the depth.

LP: Everything starts too late and when you want it, then you don't get it anymore. You get it shoved in very quickly and then you don't understand really.

ER: So an essential part of being a good therapist is your own self-development; your own extension out into the world.

LP: That's why we ask at least a decent therapy and group experience from our own therapists. It was always asked for in psychoanalysis that you have your own analysis and have worked through your main hang-ups. At least know where they are and be able to cope with them. But, beyond their professional background, I see in a lot of therapists that they know nothing, really. They know nothing of history, they know nothing of philosphy. It is what we call the humanities. We read Aristotle already in Greek in high school so when we graduated from the *gymnasium* we already had what would amount to a B.A. in classics here in America.

ER: What that reminds me of is the Aristotelian orientation of the second part, Paul Goodman's part of the book, *Gestalt Therapy*. Why is that part of the book so difficult?

LP: Is it? . . . It isn't written for uneducated people. It's written for professional people. It is not written for everybody.

ER: I'm asking the question as a "devil's advocate" because I've now been through it several times in Isadore's theory group and I have a totally different perspective on it than when I first tried to read it, some twelve years ago.

LP: You don't get it by just reading through it quickly.

ER: No.

LP: You can't take it; you can't introject it; it's quite indigestible.

ER: Was it specifically designed that way?

LP: No. It was just Paul's way of writing.

ER: Most people find it so difficult that it puts them off and they feel that there's nothing there or it's too complicated.

LP: They just haven't got the teeth, and it's unfortunate. It's not written for high school kids and most people don't get much beyond their general education. They get immediately into some type of specialty thing which remains very narrow. I think particularly as a psychologist or a therapist you have to have a wider background. Psychotherapy is as much an art as it is a science. The intuition and immediacy of the artist are as necessary for the good therapist as a scientific education.

ER: What would you like to see happen in Gestalt therapy?

LP: I couldn't even say what I would like to have happen. It's anticipating and it's pure fantasy. What I would like to happen really is that people get better training in Gestalt therapy then most of them are getting now. They think it's something that one can pick up in a week's workshop or a few weekends or something like that; and you can't. To become aware of your own process, let alone in others, and to in some way facilitate that: it takes time. Again it's biting and chewing it through. People mostly now swallow what they find intriguing in it and then they put it around and start training other people, not really knowing themselves what Gestalt really is, and what the word even means.

ER: Are you unhappy that the name stuck?

LP: No, because it's a very comprehensive thing. I wrote my approach to Gestalt in my chapter in Edward Smith's book, *The Growing Edge of Gestalt Therapy*. These are mainly the concepts that are important to me. Introjection and projection, they are really subject to the boundary concept in Gestalt therapy.

ER: Do you have more to say? I'm feeling complete about this interview at the moment.

LP: There is not much I want to say . . . What I would like to do is work that out more systematically . . .

ER: The contact and support functions?

LP: And how other concepts, which are already current in Gestalt fit into it. The contact/support concept is a Gestalt concept. Contact is always in the foreground and can fully become Gestalt and part of the ongoing Gestalt formation only when the support is ongoingly available.

ER: Aren't we back to where we started with resistance? Aren't the resistances what interrupt the contact?

LP: Resistances are what interrupt the contact and I would rather call it blocks. Resistances are fixed Gestalten. A block is a fixed Gestalt; an obsession is a fixed Gestalt. It becomes a block in the ongoing development. There is always a repetition in obsession of something that the patient doesn't get beyond.

ER: In that sense: is character bad? I think of character as fixed elements of personal style.

LP: If you read *Character Analysis* by Wilhelm Reich you know the character is a fixed formation and that it stands in place of the ongoing awareness, and, in that sense, blocks it. As a character you simply exclude certain awarenesses and certain confusions: you bypass certain experiences.

ER: True, but isn't part of that fixed formation a personal style that serves as a support for our way of being-in-the-world?

LP: But style is also something that changes, it is also subject to change. Style is really the expression of the self-development as it has happened up to that point. Hopefully the self is continually developing. The self is the integrating and integrated instance of the person while the ego is the boundary function, the temporary contact function.

ER: So when you're working with someone you're looking for the person's ability to free up some of the blocks—to take a risk.

LP: First to become aware of how they block, because it's still an activity, even if it has become automatic. Therapy is to de-automatize the blocks.

ER: First it's the awareness.

LP: Yes. First comes the awareness and then the de-automatizing and bringing it more into the foreground, exaggerating it, and out of that develops experimentation in different directions. These are the things I am working with in any workshop anywhere. My trainees are pretty much aware of the essentials. If we can't facilitate and don't facilitate the ongoing Gestalt formation, but take Gestalt therapy as a fixed method or fixed compulation of techniques, then we're dead. It's not Gestalt.

ER: Which goes back to what you were saying about the individual therapist bringing whatever he or she has . . .

LP: And every patient bringing what he or she has . . . and finding what will be possible to do with that in the actual therapeutic situation. Of course, that goes further: any relevant communication is, or can be, therapeutic in any situation. It makes a relevant change, relevant to the ongoing development which is not necessarily getting better or getting more or getting worse, but changing. Life is change. Once you stop changing you're dead.

ER: I'm writing a book about economics and there is a line in the book: "Things weren't better; things aren't better now and things will not be better in the future. Things just are."

LP: Things are and they may become different. Of course at any particular moment we may be interested in particular changes which we want to make at that point. Then again we have to see: how is that possible; what is available.

ER: In the present situation?

LP: We can only deal with what is available in the present situation and what is possible to do with what is available.

ER: One other thing occurs to me: When Freud died a lot of people felt there was a kind of scurrying around for who was going to get the ring on the merry-go-round: who would be the new head of psychoanalysis. Recently I read a quote from the book *Growth Psychology*, in the chapter on Gestalt therapy, that went something like this: "Since Fritz Perls has died, there seems to be no one who has come to take the mantle, to be the leader of Gestalt therapy." Do you think a leader is necessary? Do you think we . . .

LP: I think we need many good people. I think just *the* leader also becomes a block.

ER: In terms of people imitating a leader's style and taking that style as the whole thing?

LP: That's right. Fritz' style was imitated just in the last few years when he had narrowed it down to something he fell back on, that he had most available from earlier on. Fritz was in theater long before he did anything else. He wanted to be a theater director.

ER: A lot of hot seat work is like directing.

LP: But he also did it informed by fifty years of professional experience, which wasn't only theater. He could spot immediately people whom he could work with and people whom he knew he couldn't work with or it would be dangerous. But people who just imitate him, they are not that insightful and they often do harm; sometimes there are psychotic breaks. There are the great miracles that either die away again and not much remains of them or the so-called quick breakthrough makes for a real break.
ER: In *Garbage Pail* and *Gestalt Therapy Verbatim* Fritz is constantly denouncing the instant cure. I read into that that he was having second thoughts about what he brought about at Esalen and how dangerous it seemed to him; what he calls the joy-boys and the miracle people.
LP: That example is quite right. I feel suspicious about all the instant things: instant contact, instant intimacy, instant sex, instant something or other, instant joy. Joy is a byproduct. Happiness is a byproduct of good functioning. But suffering is also a part of creative living and working; it's not only a curse. I have written some thirty years ago, over thirty years ago, a long article on the reinterpretation of suffering, from biblical times on.
ER: Will that be part of one of your new books?
LP: Yes, I think so.
ER: Good. There is a section in Paul Goodman's novel, *The Empire City*, that Erving and Miriam Polster quote at the start of their book, *Gestalt Therapy Integrated*, where the protagonist is experiencing giving up the necessity of being totally happy:

> Soon he was softly breathing the no-geography of being at a loss. He tasted the elixir of being at a loss, when anything that occurs must necessarily be a surprise. He could no longer make any sense of his own essential things (that had never made him happy); he could feel them fleeing away from him; yet he did not snatch at them in despair. Instead he touched his body and looked around and felt, "Here I am and now," and did not become panicky.

He has the courage to go on to the next moment.
LP: You can go on from there.
ER: And know that there will be suffering, that there will be pleasure, but that I'm present, in the moment.

LP: Also, there is a certain satisfaction and maybe even momentary happiness in having lived through and overcome certain suffering during the process of development. Coping. But that's temporary and the pursuit of hapiness, per se, even if it's written in the constitution, it's a very illegitimate pursuit, it's incidental.

AN ORAL HISTORY OF GESTALT THERAPY PART TWO: A CONVERSATION WITH ISADORE FROM

Edward Rosenfeld

Continuing our series of talks with the founders, originators and developers of Gestalt therapy, The Gestalt Journal *is proud to present the second section of "An Oral History of Gestalt Therapy: A Conversation with Isadore From."*

When I first approached Laura Perls and asked her how I would go about becoming a Gestalt therapist, her suggestion was that I enter therapy with a well-grounded Gestalt therapist. She recommended Isadore From.

It took me a decade to begin my work with Isadore. Having attended his theory group and his practicum I am quite familiar with the way he teaches and trains in Gestalt therapy. For almost three decades Isadore has been taking people interested in Gestalt therapy through the rich and complex material contained in the second half of Gestalt Therapy *as well as providing a solid and imaginative model for the actual practice of psychotherapy in the Gestalt manner.*

Isadore has been active in Gestalt therapy since he first entered therapy with Frederick S. Perls. This was how we began our conversation, which took place in New York City on 14 June 1978.

ER: How did you get involved with Frederick Perls and Gestalt therapy?
IF: In 1945, I came to New York City to attend the New School for Social

Research to study with Leo Strauss, the philosopher, and William Troy—both of whom I knew about when I was in California. It became apparent after a year that I was in need of psychotherapy. Although then I think we would not have said psychotherapy—we would have said psychoanalysis. In search of a psychoanalyst with the handicap of having very little money, I failed to find one who would see me more than once a month with the amount of money I could pay.

ER: As you said before, a great many of these psychoanalysts were on Park Avenue.

IF: Yes, but then the rents on Park Avenue weren't that great an amount.

ER: But they were living very well.

IF: Yes, but what I remember is that I went to a number of analysts. I think Gardner Murphy had given me the names.

ER: He was at the New School?

IF: Yes. He gave a course in personality. In the course of this search I contacted a psychologist who agreed that I needed therapy—and quickly. He mentioned a man who had recently arrived in this country who probably needed patients and sent me to him. That man was Frederich Perls, who at that time was living in the Eighties on the East Side in a coldwater flat across from Ruppert's Brewery in NYC. This was quite a different milieu from the ones I had been visiting in my search, but the place, the way he was dressed, didn't put me off at all.

ER: But the whole atmosphere was shabby and worn down?

IF: Yes, but that did not concern me. I told him about myself and my need of a therapist. Again, I don't think I would have used the term "therapist." Analyst would have been right. He told me that he couldn't take me on as he needed full-paying patients at that time. He told me I might come back later. I remember that I said, with more courage than I might have had at that moment; "I CAN'T WAIT!" He told me that I would have to wait. Then, somehow, he asked me what I was studying. Out of my bag of studies I mentioned phenomenology. Whereupon he said; "Lie down on the couch."

ER: Were you actually well grounded in phenomenology at that time?

IF: Not at all. I had had a year's course in phenomenology. I had done some reading of Husserl. There was not much of his work available at that time in English, and I could not read German well enough to read the other material that was available. I had read some of Husserl's papers, but I didn't claim to be knowledgeable about him. I did know that I knew more than Perls did about him. And so did he. It became evident to me, later, why he was interested.

ER: Why was that?

IF: Well, if what later became Gestalt therapy has any philosophical bent, it would be from Husserl and existentialism, which is somewhat derived from his work.

ER: So upon Perls' hearing the word phenomenology, the situation changed.

IF: Yes. I lay down on the couch. He told me to describe everything that I experienced but begin each sentence with the words "here and now." That's the only thing that surprised me, as the rest of it seemed like my idea of what psychoanalysis was. He sat in back of me. I did not see him while I was on the couch.

ER: Did he talk while you were speaking? Did he have responses?

IF: I remember very little. There must have been some. But aside from two episodes, I remember no words that he said to me.

ER: What were those two episodes?

IF: Well, once he asked me did I ever have sexual fantasies about him, which kind of startled me. I got up from the couch, turned around and looked at him and said, "No, you are much too old and far too ugly." And he said, "Good, good." The second was, I had been telling him what I thought would shock anybody. He said nothing. That made me angry. I gave him more shocking details, and he said nothing. Then I angrily threw an ash tray at him and missed him. And he said, "Good, good, good." I've thought about that. I think he may have said "Good" because I missed him. And that's about all I remember that he said during the therapy sessions. I do remember things later.

ER: So you were going on a regular basis?

IF: Twice a week.

ER: For how long did you see him?

IF: A year and a half.

ER: How did the therapy terminate?

IF: He referred me to Laura Perls, his wife, who, at some time close to then had come to this country. He made it clear that I would have to work with her. I didn't know. . .

ER: And so you started therapy with Laura Perls.

IF: Yes, twice a week. The fee was the same as I had been paying—indeed very small.

ER: And was her manner of conducting therapy at all different than Frederich Perls'?

IF: Yes, in that while I lay down on a narrow couch, she sat in front of me. And, more often, made references to my breathing—which seemed unusual to me and to my friends whom I told.

ER: When you were working with Frederich Perls in the beginning you said he told you to start each sentence with the phrase "here and now."

IF: Yes.

ER: Did that continue and persist throughout your therapy with him?

IF: Yes, I think it did. I cannot actually remember it, but from what I know later in my experience with him he probably did and would have mentioned it when I got away from it.

ER: And was Laura, too, oriented toward the present?

IF: It seemed so. But less concretely. I remember her as being very much more supportive and in direct contact with me. Which at that time was a great help to me.

ER: How did the therapy with Laura terminate?

IF: I was feeling much better than when I started and I decided to terminate therapy. The only way that I knew how to at that time was to go to Europe, where I'd always wanted to go. In spite of still not having much money, I told Laura that I was going to go to Europe—which delighted her. And that ended my therapy. I went to Europe for a year and a half.

ER: And once you returned, did you have any contact with them after that?

IF: As I recall—my first actual social contact with them—it was a Thanksgiving dinner.

ER: This is after you came back from Europe?

IF: Yes. And Perls told me that he had been to California and had looked up my twin brother, who was living then and living out there. This was certainly not typical of one's therapist and maybe not ethical—to look up a patient's family. My twin brother had introduced him to a group of young psychologists in Los Angeles. And, after talking with them, he decided to move to California. He had already set up a small practice there of people who were interested in being his patients. Then the subject came up of what I was going to do—which was always a topic of my therapy, unresolved. And I said, "I don't know." As I remember, they both said, "What else can you do?" And Frederich Perls informed me that obviously I had to be a therapist and he had two patients for me from California and I would go with him.

ER: Until this point you hadn't thought of yourself as a psychotherapist or psychoanalyst or anything like that?

IF: No. Like any well-read person of the time, I would have read most of Freud, Reich certainly, somewhat less Jung. But I knew the vocabulary. It had not occurred to me that I wanted to be, or could be, a psychotherapist.

ER: But you accepted his offer.

IF: It seemed to me that I had no choice. Of course I did. But, it's true, what else could I do? He went out and I followed shortly thereafter. We shared offices in his apartment, close to Hollywood Blvd.

ER: How long were you in California?

IF: I was there approximately two years. Perls failed to be the success he thought he was going to be. And, though he certainly had an adequate practice, he left California after about a year. I took on all—most—of his patients and stayed for another year. This was during the period when *Gestalt Therapy* was about to be published. I remember the manuscript being sent to California, and I looked over particularly what became the first part, by Hefferline, and was quite unhappy with it. It seemed to me evangelical and not always interesting. As you know, Ed, the first part originally had been intended as the second part, but by editing (or so-called editing) the most it did was bring out some of the wonderful results his experiments had had. And I suggested, could we have some results that weren't so wonderful? Again, when that was sent back to Hefferline, he refused to make my changes. So it was published pretty much as he wrote it.

ER: You hadn't at this point seen the theoretical part?

IF: Yes, I saw that too. I had no quarrel with that at all. I also knew that Paul Goodman had written it.

ER: Did you know Paul Goodman?

IF: Yes, I knew Paul Goodman before I knew Perls. We had friends in common from the late thirties. I had met him once at Chicago University—I think in the late thirties. I met him through a friend, David Sachs, who was from Chicago and now teaches philosophy at Johns Hopkins. So, I had known him from the first time I had moved here to NY in 1945.

ER: When you were in Europe, or when you first returned from Europe, were you aware that Goodman was working on a theoretical part for this proposed book?

IF: Oh, yes, I knew that all along. I knew that Perls had had a somewhat sloppy manuscript, not very long (I vaguely remember reading it), and was looking for someone to put it into readable English. This happened frequently with manuscripts of his. I cannot exactly remember how Paul Goodman got involved. I do know Paul was desperately poor, as he was most of his life. Whether Perls asked him, or not, I don't know. But somehow he did take over the manuscript and in the course of writing it realized it needed much more body and wrote what became the second part. I remember his fee for that was $500.00.

ER: And that was all he ever got out of it?

IF: He was given a certain percentage of the royalties—the amount I cannot remember. At that time, there were so few sales—almost to his death there was very little more than that. Since then, due to the big sale of *Gestalt Therapy*, he, somewhat, and his estate have gotten much more. But all he expected to get, at that time, was the fee for writing the book.

ER: What do you think accounted for Goodman's really precise understanding of what has come to be the underlying theoretical structure of Gestalt therapy? There's not a lot in *Ego, Hunger and Aggression* that points to the really extensive development that he made of the whole metaphor of Gestalt and certainly the contact boundary disturbances as they are described and discussed in the second half of *Gestalt Therapy*. How did he come to that?

IF: I can't remember if I had given Paul *Ego, Hunger and Aggression* to read. I had given it to a number of my friends. They were not impressed with how it was written, and they had a lot of questions to ask about the way it was written and what was left out. I do remember discussions about that. A number of young and not so young intellectuals did become interested in *Ego, Hunger and Aggression* and realized that there was something new in it. Most of them, including Paul Goodman, would have known that Wilhelm Reich clearly influenced it. I think Goodman, more than anyone else, realized that there was a possibility of a contribution, both from Perls and the framework he had begun in *Ego, Hunger and Aggression*. Paul realized that there was a lack in that book as well as in the manuscript that Perls had given him. That lack was in bringing Freud and Wilhelm Reich together. There was also the work of Otto Rank, which at that point I don't think Perls had realized the importance of; but Paul was alert to this material. I think Goodman, in working with Perls' material, became very interested and decided to write a book of his own, but one that respected the material that Perls had provided him, which showed a particularly Gestalt therapy way of doing psychotherapy. I never heard Goodman say anything critical or abusive about the material that Perls had provided him. He might have said that it was not enough or that a lot of work had to be done. And, $500 was a lot of money then. I know it took a lot of prodding to get the money out of Perls.

ER: How did you become a therapist? Were you given any training by Perls when you went out to California or were you just thrown into the room with a patient?

IF: Sounds odd, doesn't it?

ER: Yes—you were just put in a room with a patient and told to begin?

IF: Told to begin. One of the patients he had for me was closely related to him. This, I thought, was evidence he had trust in me. And . . . we had a group, a training group in California, which consisted largely of upper-middle-class ladies. My role in that group was that of a shill in that in asking someone what they experienced, if Perls were to ask me, I would always give it in terms of "here and now" with a skill that I think some of my students today would envy. Then Perls would beam on me and at me and most of these women would then realize that "oh, this is how you're supposed to do it." (I can remember Perls would have diagrams of how Gestalten would form.) I began to emphasize the here and now more in my practice. It was an apprenticeship with only a vague presense to be an apprentice to.

ER: When you started doing therapy were you still following the psychoanalytic mode that Perls had started with you? Were you making people lie down on the couch or facing them in the way Laura had you do?

IF: Well, they did, for the most part, lie down on the couch—on a couch—but I faced them. I would say my style was more influenced by Laura than by Frederich. The fee that I received was $2.00 a session. So I didn't feel that I was gypping them out of much. Even before Perls left, my practice had already grown from the two patients that I'd started with.

ER: So you began to feel more like a real psychotherapist?

IF: Yes, though I don't think I felt like a psychotherapist for approximately 15 years.

ER: There was always some level of. . .

IF: Unease. Anxiety. "What am I doing?"

ER: What made you leave California?

IF: Well, Perls left after a year and I carried on his practice. But that's a difficult question to answer. I did not like California. I had worked for more than two years and, again, I wanted to go to Europe. So, with the $1,000 or so that I had saved I went back to Europe for another year. When I was in England I looked up, at Perls' request, a psychologist and a urino-genital specialist, both of whom had read *Gestalt Therapy* and were interested in training in it. So I stayed in London 5 or 6 months.

ER: Training those two?

IF: Yes. It mostly was therapy.

ER: And then after being in Europe for that year, you came back to America, to New York?

IF: Yes.

ER: At that point, I imagine, the N.Y. institute was already set up?

IF: Laura had started the institute near the end of Perls' first stay in California. And by the time he got there, a small group of people had been meeting at Laura's. Whether or not it was actually called an institute then I don't know. I do know that when I got back from Europe, there was stationery—New York Institute for Gestalt Therapy—and there were six or seven fellows—who were the so-called "original" fellows of the institute.

ER: Do you remember who they were?

IF: I'll try to. There was Paul Weisz, Paul Goodman, Elliot Shapiro, Frederich Perls, Laura Perls, myself, and perhaps Sylvester, better known as "Buck," Eastman. That would be it.

ER: So these were the people who were principally involved in the discussions that went on about what Gestalt therapy was?

IF: Yes. You know, it's difficult for me to put it that way. There were not, as I remember, discussions about what it was. They were, I think, to begin with, group meetings. Goodman was probably the most active. There were discussions, but certainly I can't remember there being a topic about "what Gestalt therapy was." There were frequent exchanges—differences—I wouldn't say quarrels—but differences. But the important thing that I would like to emphasize is—no one was regarded as "the Biggie." None of them. Frederich Perls, Laura Perls . . .

ER: Paul Goodman?

IF: Paul Goodman, Paul Weisz, myself, anybody. I think, in a real sense, that I was less qualified. We did regard each other as peers.

ER: When did you start going out to Cleveland?

IF: That, I think, must have been about 1952.

ER: Was this upon your return from your second trip to Europe?

IF: Shortly after. Now, as I remember it, 2 or 3 psychologists came to New York. They had heard of our so-called institute, and attended. They went back to Cleveland and gathered 5 or 6 other clinical psychologists and asked Perls to come there. That was the first of such "traveling" trips. He went there. And, I think it was the second visit, perhaps two or three months later, when they had gathered a few more people, that Paul Weisz and myself went with him. We were in small groups and with individuals. I think Paul Weisz and I went twice with Perls. And Paul and I were quite distressed at what we observed. What happened was indeed dramatic, but neither one of us could appreciate that it was therapy. It was a lot of shaking, trembling, anxiety—which I didn't understand. And Paul Weisz, who was a physician, told me he thought "Perls was getting these dramatic results as a result of hyperventilation." This was the first I knew about hyperventilation and I've never forgotten it. Also, what I observed on the second visit was that the difficulties that had emerged on the first visit merely repeated themselves in an exaggerated form. Also, differences between people were, somehow, being encouraged by what we had been doing. And I, somewhat angrily, with Perls at lunch (Paul Weisz was also there) told him that I thought what we were doing was irresponsible and that if we were going to be teaching Gestalt therapy—or training—these people would need a therapist they could see regularly and not on this every-now-and-then basis. Whereupon Perls agreed with me, readily, and said that I would be coming there.

ER: So that's how it was decided that you would become the regular trainer of the Cleveland Institute?

IF: Yes. Then he informed these people that I would be coming there. That made me uneasy. First of all, most of these people were very well-trained psychologists—all of them. Why should they take me, whose background was quite different than theirs, and take me on the orders of Perls? And they did. But I made it quite clear that this was on a trial basis. That lasted 5 years, twice a month—and then 5 more years, once a month, and at least once or twice a year since then.

ER: A long time.

IF: In the process I learned a great deal.

ER: I know the way you conduct your training now; you have trainees work with you for at least one year going through, almost line by line, the theoretical, or second-half, Paul Goodman section of *Gestalt Therapy*. Were you using that as a primary text when you were first going out to Cleveland and training people there?

IF: Oh, yes. We did exactly that. There was a theory group where we met and discussed *Gestalt Therapy* as well as a therapy group. I was seeing each person about four times a month, in those two groups and individually. We could treat difficulties with the text with the understanding that they might also be problems in their therapy; what is stopping this person from understanding this section. I could use the text in the therapy. Not that I insisted that they take the text as holy writ, but it was interesting to assume that a difficulty of understanding, when reading the text, might be the difficulty of the reader and that might be worth working through. Then we could also criticize the text.

ER: What made you change that approach?

IF: Well, partly, many of the people I see in training now I do not see in individual therapy; I see them only in theory group or in my practicum.

ER: Why do you think no one else has ever done important theoretical work since the publication of *Gestalt Therapy*? Or has tried to expand on what Paul Goodman has done?

IF: You know, I'm somewhat uneasy about the word "theory." I use it a lot, too. What I think Paul Goodman did was to make articulate that which was not articulated. It was an articulation of what a Gestalt therapist *does*, not simply what to do. In that sense it's an explanation of what a Gestalt therapist, if he thought about it, or had reasoned it out, would say to explain to others what he does. Therefore there is not that separation of theory from practice. But the great contribution, the truly great contribution that Perls made, was in the realm of *introjection*. It was greater than he himself realized. Paul Goodman recognized it. That was the area of Perls' important difference with Freud. The implication for the writer of a text, and I think Goodman recognized this, was that a serious text could not be written if it risked being introjected by the reader. What we insist on calling the theoretical is a way of writing about this serious matter, Gestalt therapy, in a way that reasonably prevents introjection.

ER: What is the danger of introjecting the theory or of introjecting the description of what is done in Gestalt therapy?

IF: The dangers have been realized, to a certain extent. In the last ten years we have unknowledgeable imitators who are introjectors of, most importantly I think, Perls in his later years. They are not sufficiently critical of themselves or others. The danger is that, without being aware of it, they have abandoned one of the grounds of Gestalt therapy: that our patients are not to introject us.

ER: How does this differ from other therapies? Say, psychoanalysis?

IF: In a serious psychoanalytic therapy to introject the analyst was not undesirable. To accept the interpretations of the analyst by introjecting, uncritically, is not regarded as unhealthy. Not to accept them, or to be unable to, is regarded as a resistance. They have perfectly good theoretical and practical reasons for that. It is Perls' insight into what he thought was a mistake of Freud's about the healthy period of introjection that makes the Gestalt therapist more cautious about the possibility of introjecting practical or theoretical matters. What you've got is a serious quarrel with Freud. Freud regarded introjection as being healthy until a relatively late age. And Perls, because of his interest in teeth and how we had been ignoring them . . .

ER: The whole vista of dental aggression . . .

IF: Yes. But that one insight really opened the door—made a new therapy necessary. So you can see why a book on Gestalt therapy that risks being introjected is a violation of Gestalt therapy.

ER: I guess what I'm getting at is that so much of what we see now that's called Gestalt therapy is really a demonstration style rather than a way of doing therapy.

IF: Yes, which is what Perls did the last years of his life—gave demonstrations or small vignettes of Gestalt therapy. He did not do Gestalt therapy. You cannot do therapy in 15 or 20 minutes.

ER: So you think that's a primary difference then—that he was working in this "short-time" format.

IF: He was interested in influencing large bodies of people. And, he did that successfully. Only if people will remember the context of it—again another crucial concept of Gestalt therapy—they might realize that you cannot do the same thing with small groups, individuals, or with certain problems. But, for the *context*, what Perls did might have been adequate. But those of us who use that method in another context—we have not made the necessary changes.

ER: You mentioned earlier that you felt that some of the basis for what started in *Ego, Hunger and Aggression* and later became known as Gestalt therapy came from the works certainly of Freud. You also mentioned phenomenology and existentialism and the works of Reich and Rank. I think some of the influences of Reich and certainly Freud have been delineated in a variety of different works. I wonder if you would make some comments about Otto Rank's contribution?

IF: Yes. It was Paul Goodman who recognized that either directly or indirectly, Perls had been influenced by Rank. When Perls was in Europe, Rank was not unknown. And his differences with Freud were known. I later learned that it was Otto Rank who first used the expression "here and now." He was the first to emphasize the possibility that concentrating on the present might indeed by very useful. He did not extend that to the extent that Perls did. But he certainly thought of it. Otto Rank was also, I learned later, the first to suggest what Perls rediscovered (Perls had the talent for discovering what he'd already discovered again, and again. And he was not lying—it was always, for him, a new discovery, slightly formulated another way). It was Otto Rank who suggested that it would be useful to consider every element of the dream a projection. Which, later I think, Perls announces as a discovery of his. And again, I'm sure that's how he experienced it. The influence that Rank had on Goodman is evident in the text of *Gestalt Therapy*.

ER: Where he makes references to *Art & Artists*.

IF: Yes, and almost with as much grace as he does to *The Interpretation of Dreams*. Goodman had read all the available Rank, really—there wasn't much, but he'd read with great care *Art & Artists*, which to this day I find it extremely difficult to get through.

ER: Me, too.

IF: But that touched Goodman a great deal and it was not irrelevant to bring that into the foreground in writing *GT*.

ER: You have an approach to working with dreams that, from what I understand of it, differs significantly from the Freudian symbolic approach to dreams as well as from what I might call the Perlsian existential approach to dreams. I was wondering if you could summerize, at least briefly, how you work with dreams and how you look at the importance of the dream in a therapy session.

IF: You know, I get a bit uneasy with the word "existential." I would suspect that the way I use dreams is as existential as Perls' use of dreams. I wouldn't make that claim about how I use dreams. It's an uneasy-making word these days. It is not a different approach; it is "in addition to." What Perls seemed to suggest was that the best way to deal with dreams—or perhaps the only way—was to consider all the elements of the dream as a projection and, in the therapy, to seek out the projections and work at assimilating them. As I recall, this is largely done by the use of the empty seat and the patient attempting to become the part of the dream which the therapist would have selected as the important projection in the dream. I have no quarrel with that. I do think it is often not sufficient. What I think I've added is: what if we consider a dream a retroflection. An "unawares" retroflection is, of course, one of the important disturbances at the contact boundary which have always been of interest, particularly in Gestalt therapy. Now, there's nothing particularly new about what Perls says about dreams. I'm not so sure there's anything particularly new about what I say. Otto Rank made the same suggestion about dreams many years before. It is true that it was largely neglected until Perls mentioned it. The important dreams, if you're going to consider the dream as an unawares retroflection, would be the dream the night after therapy and the dream the night before therapy. There is no way of proving this. But one can, at least, try it, which I have done—and others have done—and discover that it has important value in bringing out disturbances at the contact boundary of the patient and the therapist. The presumption that I'm working on is that a dream is a retroflection par excellence, because one dreams when one sleeps and all contact, except breathing, is given up. So, if you consider a dream also as an attempt to undo retroflections that may have occurred during a therapy session, you may contact material that would otherwise be neglected—or you will contact it more economically. By that I mean you'll save time. It is a fact that a patient in therapy usually knows that if he remembers a dream he will be telling it to his therapist. Therefore I assume that fact might determine, somewhat, what that patient dreams. It isn't only a dream, it is a dream that he will be telling his therapist. So this could be his attempt to contact and undo retroflections that reflect disturbances at the contact boundary with his therapist.

ER: I can understand that totally in terms of the dream that occurs the night before the therapy session . . .

IF: That would be the night after it also.

ER: Well, what you were saying before was that the dream is something that the patient will discuss with the therapist and I can see the patient remembering the dream from the night before the therapy session and bringing it up the next day as part of therapy. What I'm confused about is the dream the night after the therapy session when perhaps there will be a week or several days time elapsing. I understand that it might be a retroflection, but I wonder if that dream is dreamed quite so significantly in order to tell the therapist or as something that would be told.

IF: Well, therapy usually is an ongoing process and the fact that there is a session within a few days or a week is also known to the dreamer/patient. The reason I suggest that the dream of the night after therapy might be an important one in undoing retroflections is that the retroflections would have occurred during that session. Another name for retroflections would be censoring—withholding—the patient's talking to himself—saying to himself during a session things that he could not, or would not, say to the therapist. I think you will discover if you concentrate on this in working with the dream after a session that the patient will repeat something of significance somewhere in the dream—for example the word "foolish" might appear strongly in the dream the night after a session. The therapist might say to the patient. "How was I foolish at our last session?" Frequently enough the patient might, with some difficulty, point to something that the therapist said or did that he was unable to discuss during the session. Those disturbances often interfere with therapy if they are not said—in this case the criticism by the patient of the therapist. In the dream he is in essence saying it again to himself. But I am presuming that the fact that he does that in the dream would suggest he is ready to undo this retroflection and would be able to openly criticize—i.e., differ with—his therapist within the session. He did not know, nor would the therapist have known, that there was that material. Does that answer part of it?

ER: Sure.

IF: I'm not saying only the dream of the night after or the night before. But those, I think, often prove the most valuable. I regularly, in orienting my patients, tell them I am particularly interested in the dream of the night before or the night after. Of course telling them that places a premium on those dreams for the patient and understandably he or she is more likely to remember them. But, I emphasize, not only those dreams. Any dream the patient might tell me, I will first consider it in this way. The dream of the night before is more valuable in determining where to go next in the therapy. It is as if a rehearsal, which is a form of retroflecting. In the waking state the patient often plans what to talk to his or her therapist about. In the dream of the night before (particularly but not only) the patient may be doing something similar. In this case he may be considering profounder material than he would have otherwise. And it is an attempt of the patient to give instructions to the therapist about the state of the therapy, emphasizing less the problems of the contact of the patient with the therapist. Do you understand the difference?

ER: I'm wondering if you have an example that might illustrate this.

IF: At a workshop a psychiatrist (after having met me, of course—therefore I could presume the dream would have to do with me and not what he had heard about me.) dreams of a messy office. Looking at this person, it did not seem conceivable to me that he was capable of having a messy office. And, if I remember the dream correctly, he berates, very angrily, his nurse for the messy office. My first question was, "How was I messy yesterday?" With some difficulty, namely embarrassment, he was able to tell me that I dressed messily—which was true—and that this was disturbing to him. There was no reason why it shouldn't be. And until he could tell me that and experience that I didn't get angry myself, he could not trust me. Then we got to the anger in the dream. What we were able to contact was his conception of anger. It turned out that what anger meant to him was murderousness. I would not have known that in the brief meeting that I had with that person in a group—a stranger—but in the dream, having been able to pick out the episode of the anger of the figure of himself at his nurse, we could contact a problem which might have taken much longer to get to if we had not dealt with the dream in this way. In this lucky case it turned out that withholding anger had indeed been very important to him and now he knew what was behind that: that if anger meant murder, then indeed, he would have to withhold it. He did not know that's how he experienced anger. That's about as much as I could say about that. Now, of course, that's taking one dream and making it work both ways. In this case I only saw this person two times.

ER: Do you ever work with dreams in the way Perls did, at least in his demonstrations, by having people actually play out parts, persons, objects and so forth as though they were those parts, persons, or objects?

IF: That, as I think I said earlier, was his attempt to assimilate projections. I prefer—I won't say never—I rarely use the empty seat because I keep the contact of the patient and myself—in so far as it's possible—always in the foreground. I would have the patient talk to me about what he feels when he tries to experience himself as one of these feelings. I would merely add that I would insist that the patient be aware that he is telling me about that feeling, not becoming it. In this case not telling it *to* the therapist often turns it into an acting exercise.

ER: In the empty chair technique, someone is talking to empty space as though it were their parent or sibling. You, in dream work as well as in the rest of therapy, try and orient the therapy toward the contact between you and the patient rather than the patient and some imaginary figure?

IF: I would more often say, "tell this to me as if I were your parent." I think both are useful. It's clear, you see, what I'm more interested in is transferential material. And the other technique is more interested in becoming aware of and attempting to undo the projection.

ER: Do you see transferential material as playing a big part in Gestalt therapy?

IF: I hear your quizzical tone, Ed. Indeed. It is because of the transference, which Freud discovered (he did not invent), that we are able to emphasize "here and now." The transference is the equivalent of "here and now," and it is this discovery of Freud's that made psychotherapy possible.

ER: So then transference becomes the grounds not just for Freudian psychoanalysis but for any kind of therapy in terms of the present situation.

IF: It makes it possible for unfinished situations of the past, which any therapy has to deal with, to be finished *presently*. Because of what Freud calls transference, the present continues to be unawares influenced by these unfinished situations of the past. How this is done is what we emphasize in Gestalt therapy.

ER: Through the contact boundary . . .

IF: Yes.

ER: Interruptions and disturbances . . .

IF: Particularly projections. We do not *encourage* the transference, as is reasonably done in psychoanalysis because of the method. But that we do not encourage it does not mean that we eliminate it. I am saying—suggesting—that it is absurd to say that we don't use transference. We would rarely use that word. We might be asking such questions as "How am I like your father?" "How am I like your mother?" Those questions, which are common enough in Gestalt therapy, are in fact questions attempting to alert our patient to transference and to undo the transference. I think the word "transference" for us might be wrong. We might say "transferring."

ER: In order to make it more process oriented?

IF: Yes. And *how* that is done.

ER: Before, you mentioned, when talking about dreams, that you orient your patients toward being alert to the dream of the night before or the night after the therapy session, and that brings me to at least a few questions about beginnings and endings in therapy. Would you share some of the ways in which you orient a patient in terms of starting therapy?

IF: It's easier to tell you about beginnings than it is about endings.

ER: That's why I started at the beginning.

IF: I think orienting the patient is often neglected. I tell the person who comes to see me how I work, what I'm interested in. I might say something like "Everything you experience here in this room, *with me*, is relevent and important." This is the equivalent of telling the patient that what we're concentrating on is the present and the present contact with me since, in individual therapy, we will be the only two persons in the room. An important part of the way I work is that—not that the patient is talking or saying something, not that only, but that he is saying something, telling something, *to me*. Then I inform him that what he remembers is also happening *at this time*. That that is how the past is made present in therapy: it is by remembering. Whether it is remembering what he did the day before or on the way to his therapy session or twenty years before. But the remembering is the *present* activity and telling it to me is the *next* present activity. At that point I might say, "And if you remember your dream, I would ask you to tell it to me." I am not saying the patient *should* remember the dream, I am informing the patient that it is useful *if* he does. I do not ask the patient to make any *special* effort, because it is important to see what the patient will *do* about it—about remembering. And I might say, "*I* am particularly interested in your dreams of the night before a session and the night after." That is not saying I'm not interested in the others.

ER: It seems, so far, that in the way you orient a patient, you bring what happens in the therapy in as the present tense of what's going on in "the here-and-now." And also you instruct a patient that what is remembered is also a present process. That the remembering *is* the present process. I'm wondering how, if at all, you work with the future, paranoia, fantasies, rehearsals.

IF: Concern with the future is a present activity. It is planning, anticipating, preparing. In otherwords, preparing, planning, anticipating, is what is going on in the present. I'm as interested in the planning, the anticipating, etc., as much as I am its content. Neither is irrelevant. I would want my patient to be aware that he or she is anticipating—leaving the session—going somewhere—and telling me about his or her anticipation. The present activity is anticipating.

ER: Frederich Perls often described maturity as the transition from environmental support to self-support, and I am curious what you look for once you've been working with someone for awhile that indicates to you that some assimilation of the therapy is taking place and perhaps the end of therapy is approaching.

IF: That's a more difficult question to try to answer. And I think the reason for that, Ed, is that the beginnings of therapy are much more simple than the endings. Just as neurotic behavior is notorious for being predictable, healthy behavior is equally notorious for not being predictable; so it does make sense to say I can tell you more about the beginning than the endings because the endings for one person would be quite different than for another. I think, as Goodman put it, when you're both agreed that the patient is aware that it is he or she that walks into my room and he or she that talks to me—which would mean an absence of projections, introjections, retroflections, then the therapy is through.

ER: Not during this interview, but at other times we have talked about assimilation and the role of assimilation in therapy, and one of the comments you made on one occasion was that "oftentimes real assimilation, in terms of therapy, takes place, actually, outside the therapy."

IF: I would say inevitably. Now by outside the therapy I do not mean that there isn't assimilation going on during the period when therapy is going on—but I mean outside the therapy *room* or the therapy *meeting* with the therapist. During the week—let us say there is a week between sessions—some assimilation ought to occur. I do not think the insight or the "ahah" is the actual assimilation. To use the example of food, the feeling, the hunger, beginning to see food in the environment, going to get it, taking it, bringing it to your mouth, chewing it, swallowing it, are awares activities. The actual assimilation of food is not awares. Similarly, intellectual assimilation is not awares, or emotional assimilation (if we can use that term). When something I have heard becomes *mine*, I'm aware of that. When it becomes *me*, I am not. The "ahah" might be the moment of awareness—that *this is mine*. Now, that this becomes me is not an awares process. That's why I say that assimilation must go on between sessions and certainly *after* a successful therapy. That is why when I take a vacation I am not surprised that some patients do very well and, in a sense, are better with my absence than if we had continued meeting. It provides me with a vacation and them with a vacation from ongoing therapy, which might be providing time to assimilate what had been going on during the therapy. I think it's also why we have to be careful crediting ourselves with what in fact are the success of others. A patient going from one therapy, or one school of therapy, to another—the second therapist or school of therapy may be enjoying that which has been assimilated from the previous therapy or therapist.

ER: Do you have any speculations at all as to the absence of criticism within the Gestalt community of Gestalt therapy per se? Most of the literature that is published, in terms of books and the few papers on Gestalt therapy, seems mostly to be expository—or in some way championing Gestalt therapy.

There are very, very few, certainly in writing, criticisms I've seen of Gestalt therapy. Any speculations as to what causes that?

IF: That's extremely difficult for me to answer. It does not seem familiar to me, since I am all too aware of my own limitations and the present limitations of what I would call Gestalt therapy. So, if that's what you mean by criticism, I am critical of the limitations and that is what interests me. Whatever successes I have had in therapy, practicing Gestalt therapy, are of relatively little interest to me. What failures, or disappointments, I have had do interest me. In teaching I emphasize our limitations. I am not an evangelist, and I have never thought of Gestalt therapy as having the answer to all the problems of psychotherapy. I think we could use much more examination of ourselves and or method. I think what has caused or would seem to have caused this is too much introjection and not enough criticism. I think I could say that some of us may have been guilty of urging and enabling others to introject. I think what I'm referring to is the style of, let us say, *Gestalt Therapy Verbatim*—the style encourages the reader's introjecting and minimizes criticism from the reader. The style of *Gestalt Therapy* by Perls, Hefferline, and Goodman does the reverse. It discourages, almost makes impossible, introjection.

ER: And yet that book at this point is 28 years old and I guess what my first question was referring to, which in part you've answered, is that very few people are willing to be public with what criticisms they have of Gestalt therapy—what limitations they sense in Gestalt therapy. The only one that I remember, in writing, was Mary Henle, who is not a Gestalt therapist, criticizing Gestalt therapy in terms of its connections with Gestalt psychology. But I don't remember seeing much else in writing.

IF: Interestingly enough, what she criticizes is *Gestalt Therapy Verbatim*. And, quite rightly says that Perls is presumed to have said that everything before that was obsolete. She wasn't intellectually obliged to criticize what had been acknowledged as obsolete. I think she would have had more difficulty with that if she had concentrated her criticism on *Gestalt Therapy* and not *Gestalt Therapy Verbatim*. That there isn't more criticism suggests that not enough serious people are familiar with Gestalt therapy.

ER: Do you have at the tip of your tongue a few limitations of Gestalt therapy—things that you come up against in your own practice and your own training of people—that are particular to Gestalt therapy?

IF: Well, I may have them at the tip of my tongue, but in trying to answer them I am tongue-tied. Yes, I have many, many questions about "what next in Gestalt therapy." I have never believed that Gestalt therapy has solved all of the problems. I think, often it is more efficient—certainly not always—than other therapies. I do not think it is efficient enough. Often we make it seem as if Gestalt therapy is always of short duration. And the record simply will not support it.

AN ORAL HISTORY OF GESTALT THERAPY PART THREE: A CONVERSATION WITH ERVING AND MIRIAM POLSTER

Joe Wysong

We continue with our oral history of the development of Gestalt therapy with an interview with Erving and Miriam Polster. Probably best known for their book, Gestalt Therapy Integrated, *published in 1973, both have been active in Gestalt therapy almost since its inception and were a part of the first Gestalt "study" group started outside New York City. From this group evolved The Gestalt Institute of Cleveland, which just celebrated its 25th Anniversary.*

Active in the Cleveland Institute for almost 20 years, the Polsters left Cleveland and moved to California where they established The Gestalt Training Center—San Diego. In addition to their programs in San Diego, Erv and Miriam travel, both separately and together, throughout the country conducting training workshops and seminars for other institutions.

Last fall, Erv and Miriam Polster were conducting a five day training workshop on Cape Cod. What follows is condensed from a conversation that began after lunch, was interrupted by an afternoon training session, and then continued until early evening and dinner.

Erv and I began the interview alone, and were joined at a later point (indicated in the text) by Miriam. Our conversation took place on October 19, 1978 in Provincetown, Massachusetts.

JW: What were you doing professionally when you first heard of Fritz Perls and Gestalt Therapy?
EP: I had gotten my Ph.D. from Western Reserve three years earlier in 1950. I already had two years on the faculty of the University of Iowa, half teaching and half clinical work. I came back to Cleveland in '51 and started a private practice and was also doing some supervisory work at the University. I was Director of Psychotherapy in the Psychology Department at Cleveland State Hospital, where I did some early group therapy work. In 1953 Marjorie Creelman called me about a workshop that Fritz was doing in Cleveland. They'd already had one, and this was the second one. I went. I just was very aroused and re-oriented. Not re-oriented, but more fully oriented about what I was doing and thinking. Everthing seemed to come together more clearly, seeing what Fritz was doing and saying. I also needed further training. I'd been out of graduate school for four years. I'd gone about as far as I felt I could go on what I had learned in graduate school and to get some new inspiration and new training was very important to me. There was not much that was available because in those days we didn't have the same kind of diverse training that exists today outside graduate schools.
JW: Is there anything from that first workshop with Fritz that's particularly vivid to you?
EP: I don't remember any specific content, but I do remember the power of seeing someone have a profound personal experience in a group of people who had not previously been intimate. That was a revelation to me. It wasn't done much then. Nowadays it's taken for granted, but then to see somebody say something that was so powerful they would cry, right there among fifteen people from the community who were not related to them, who were not necessarily even their friends; was a revelatory experience.
JW: Did the group only meet when Perls came to Cleveland?
EP: No. We met leaderless weekly. We did a lot of exploration that was novel for us in those days. Explorations of how we walked, how we talked, how we saw, how we used our language and much more. That lasted a year and a half. We also had workshops with Fritz about four times a year. We also had many workshops with Paul Weisz, and some with Laura. The first workshop was with Fritz and Paul Weisz—they came jointly. After a while, Paul got tired of being seen as a couple with Fritz, and wanted to be invited on his own, so we invited him separately. Soon, Paul Goodman came in. We

had a lot of trouble getting Paul in through Fritz. He felt like Paul would be too much for us, or he thought Paul would be an enfant terrible—but we wanted to meet with Paul, because we knew of him as co-authoring the book, *Gestalt Therapy*. We did, finally, meet with Paul. We met with him quite a lot.

JW: At what point did Isadore start his visits to Cleveland?

EP: Isadore came to one of the early workshops that Fritz and Paul did together, around 1955. Soon Isadore began working with us individually. We knew we needed more than we could get from workshops. We wanted somebody from New York to come in to work with us individually. Isadore was available. First he came in twice a month and he'd stay for a few days each time, so that each one of us could get a couple of sessions with him twice a month. We didn't know him very well before we started to work with him, but we came to know him very intimately. He came in for about four years on a once a month basis, then he went off to live in Europe for a couple of years. When he came back to this country he came back to Cleveland again for a couple of years.

JW: I'd enjoy some brief impressions of Perls, Paul Goodman, Paul Weisz and Laura Perls as they were at the time.

EP: It's very difficult. I can't do it without a disclaimer about my facility about my doing it right. From Fritz I got the realization that a person could have incredible range in characteristics. I could experience Fritz as the most cutting and the most tender of all people. I loved that contrast.

JW: You saw this both in his work and in him as an individual?

EP: I'm talking about his work. Outside of his work there was a very different quality between us. In his work I felt his power of creating tension to be greater than any I've ever seen. A tension that was lively—at any moment the world would change. He got across that kind of vibrancy of life. And he would get across a sense of courage to be able to go into any undercurrent trip. It was as though one were to go on an LSD trip (LSD was not known in those days) and he would always be there. There was no way that he wouldn't know what to do on that trip. I was incredibly supported and inspired to be able to take some of the trips that I took with him. He was a man of vast power to assimilate what somebody was saying to him, no matter how large it was. You would say something large to him, and he'd be just as large. You could say something small and he could stoop to hear it.

He had this great range—and he had an X-ray quality. I suddenly discovered that a person could actually know another person for the moment without knowing them wholly. He seemed a genius to me. I'd never known a genius first hand. I'd read about them. Now I felt like I'd met a genius before the critics got to him. I was able to feel that without anybody having said it to me about him. I really loved having the opportunity to know my own mind about that without having heard a lot of stories about him . . . I could get it fresh. I was so entranced with the way he functioned that I used to immitate his way of smoking. I would even find myself saying *yes* as though I had some remote contact with being German. It was very strange, I could hardly believe myself when I did it. I got over that, but I was entranced. He was a man who could cast spells.

JW: I think it's important that you're talking about 1952 or 1953 because now we hear a lot about immediacy and presence, but in that context, at that time. . . .

EP: Yes. I used to watch him work with people. One time he worked with a person who came in for a demonstration, who was not in our group. Every step of the way he went I could think of things I would say that would carry the process further . . . from interpretation . . . to general knowing of the person . . . but he didn't. He got into that person each moment. That was enough for him. And of course that accumulated into a very large experience.

JW: And Paul Weisz?

EP: Paul Weisz came at the same time as Fritz. Sometimes he came with Fritz, sometimes he came separately. Paul Weisz was a very different man. He was, first of all, a man of finer steps. He would take small steps in therapy. He could move with a person from one sensation to the next where Fritz wouldn't do that. And you had a feeling with Paul of almost Zen knowing when he would have difficulty verbalizing. He was not as simple in his verbalizations as Fritz. Fritz could describe what he wanted to describe as long as he didn't have to talk longer than a paragraph. He could talk with exquisite clarity, using figures of speech and very simple language. He could talk to you as though he was telling a story to a child. With great resonance in his voice and with profound content. Paul was much more abstract in his talking. It was a little harder for us to get the words from him, but he was incredibly sensitive about whatever was happening and he had the deepest respect for a person's creative process. I had a feeling that I could go anywhere with Paul. He wasn't the inspirational force that Fritz was. When you were done with Fritz, you might have been Svengalied into what you got in to. But Paul Weisz was not a Svengali man. He was a very human, brave, responsible man. He was the kind of person who could love something you'd done even though it wasn't obvious that everybody would love it, or even if it was trite—he saw the beauty in it. He could respond in a way that would get to the beauty instead of the triteness. He was physically more vigorous than Fritz, though not as graceful. He was younger. He introduced a Zen experience into our situation. I remember being silent with him for hours. It was the first time I'd ever experienced the power of a silent experience. Paul wasn't invoking silence. He was not a man to invoke things. I remember doing an experiment which was very eye-opening. He brought a pail of water. The idea was to immerse our heads in it. And breathe. I don't remember the experience exactly . . . it's been so long. But I remember feeling the power of how I could, through self-experimentation, change that which was simply a pail of water into a microcosm of life. He had a way of doing that. I remember putting my head into that water and remembering the moment of the expansion of all my sensations and anxiety into excitement at the prospect of drowning. As though I could have drowned right there in that little pail of water. I was taking that chance in life. I came out of it alive, having a sense for the microcosmic quality. It was that sort of thing that Paul Weisz introduced me to.

JW: And he wasn't getting it from books.

EP: No. In fact, Isadore had introduced me to a book called *Zen and the Art of Archery*. There wasn't much Zen around. Obviously there were philosophers who knew a lot about Zen, but when I say not much Zen around, I mean it was through Paul and somewhat through Fritz that we could get a sense of how the Eastern systems and the Western systems were merging. Meeting, if not merging.

JW: What about Isadore?

EP: Isadore was a very different person. At first we were all in individual therapy with him. Then, we had theory meeting with him in small groups. The way we did theory with Isadore was to read *Gestalt Therapy* together. Each of us would take a turn reading it. We would stop the reader at a time when we wanted to ask a question. I can remember some of the questions that I was concerned with, that I needed further explanation for, and would disagree about, and that Isadore would explain. It was a new idea that happiness might not be the major goal in life. I would argue that point with Isadore. I probably still might argue that point. But whether I would agree or disagree is not as important to me as what he further accentuated for me. I said, all we care about is to feel good. His position was that to feel as you feel is more what life is about, irrespective of whether one was happy or not happy—irrespective of your feeling. Function came across as transcending questions of feeling good or feeling happy. There were many discussions of that sort. They were pretty intellectual discussions, which has not always been harmonious with the Gestalt view. Still isn't. I think that's changing. One of the important things for me in my later development was deciding to go back to the concepts. That's when I started the first course I did in Cleveland on the concepts of Gestalt therapy where I wanted to deal with the *concepts* of the method rather than the *experience* of the method. That was a blast for me. What I have come to develop as my perspectives on Gestalt therapy are a result of that first course. I newly organized the concepts to present them to the people in Cleveland. An interesting thing happened during the time I was doing the lecturing. It was just totally lecture and discussion. One day Fritz came to town and said, "What are you doing these days?" And I said, "Well, I'm teaching a course in Gestalt therapy from the standpoint of concepts. I'm also doing experiential things, but I want this to be just concepts." And he said, "That's fantastic, I'm interested in that too, and I'm starting to write and I would like to come and present something to your class." So I said to him, "Well, I would love you to do that Fritz, *if* you'll do that—*not to be experiential.*" He said, "Yes, yes, yes, yes, yes. That's just what I want to do. I want to do it, and I want a place to do it, and this is the place." So he came and gave a lecture for about five minutes. You could see his mind beginning to falter in the lecture form. Not falter, that isn't the right way to put it, but—as though he would not be able to elaborate fully and felt compelled to show how to do what he was talking about. So he started working with somebody and the rest of the session was a magnificent experience. No more concepts. Because Fritz was a man of aphorism, wry sayings; not a man of extended conceptualizations, of dealing with the obvious contradictions and the obvious implications, the obvious additions to what he might be saying.

JW: That leaves us with Paul Goodman and Laura. . . .

EP: I want to say more about Isadore. First of all, he was more intimate with us. He knew us better. Second of all, he had a certain learnedness about him that Fritz and Paul didn't bring into the picture. Paul was a learned man—Paul Weisz I'm talking about now. But Paul Weisz didn't bring it in much. What he knew was usually brought in through his integration of it, rather than as the original. Isadore was at the borderline of the writer-artist and the therapist. I had more of the feeling of the relationship of the artist to the therapist when I was with Isadore than I did with either of the others. In fact, one of my more anxious moments in therapy with Isadore was at a point when I was doing some magnificent things in my own therapy. They felt artful, and I began to feel something of what the relationship was between the artist and the therapist. Then I suddenly realized that my art form might be to be the patient. That alarmed me to no end (laughs). But in any case, there was that with Isadore. And then, with Isadore, we had continuity. Isadore did not run a medicine man act, in the sense of the magic potion. I'm not saying that the magic potions were not valuable, because I think some of the magic potions were very revealing. I loved them, and find them very educational. They just need the substance of the continuing. Isadore gave us that substance and continuity. And in the years that we were with him we just flowered. I really should speak about myself now. *I* flowered. I discovered ways of existing that would not even have been fantasies for me as a graduate student. And I say that without being modest, because I was an excellent graduate student and I was seen as doing excellent work when I got out of graduate school. I came to Gestalt therapy from the position of the excellence of the profession of that day, into a new day, where there were new illuminations that the profession just didn't know about. I was also young, and ripe, and it was very timely for me to grow in that direction. I felt that Isadore's sensitivity was a very un-stereotypic sensitivity. For example, I hardly remember Isadore ever asking me to do anything that I would not be able to do. It's as though he followed my position so perfectly; so finely, that when he would ask me to do something, it was right there to do it. And I wondered for a number of years how it was that my patients wouldn't be as ready as I was with him, and I discovered from him something of how experience enters into the ju-jitsu moment when the right timing happens, when something can be said very easily that *leads* into eruption, it doesn't *force* eruption. Actually with Isadore it's more like releasing a bird. I got that from his patience with me—his sensitivity for every step of my development—for his letting me go my own route.

JW: And Paul Goodman?

EP: Paul came after I was already in individual therapy with Isadore. Paul was simply and beatifically outrageous. He was a combination of the beatific and the outrageous—it was simple for him. He was an inspiration for me. He was an incredibly curious man. He was more curious about the person he was working with than interested in whether there would be a cure. I picked up a lot of that curiosity. And he enjoyed a good joke. all these people were funny people, but there was something special with Paul about a good joke. I mean, Fritz would *tell* a joke, but Paul would *savor* a joke. He would love the deliciousness of the relationship of one experience to another. And he would be bemused as well as amused. He would laugh, but he would always feel the human condition in the joke. It was not only a joke but also a poem. Paul Goodman really could not understand how anybody could do less than *he* could do.

JW: Was Goodman working with the book as Isadore was?

EP: No. He was more like a street philosopher than a Gestalt theoretician. The people in Cleveland, as I observed, were never as taken with Paul as a workshop leader as I was. If Paul came in for a workshop, he didn't get the same turnout. Even after he had written *Growing Up Absurd*. Some of us were just panting to be with him, but it didn't turn out.to be as festive a thing as some of the other workshops. I never understood that. Goodman did not create the tension system that either Fritz or Paul Weisz did. He was not a man to create a tension system. He was a man of conversation. He was a man of story-telling. He was occasionally provocative. He liked hearing stories. You might have someone in the room telling a story, and the other people might be bored, but *he* was fascinated. And he liked to tell stories. But, I think these days, one needs to think in terms of tight sequentiality and loose sequentiality . . .

JW: What do you mean by "sequentiality?"

EP: Well, one of my simple rules of therapy is that one thing follows another. Now that's a very simple rule, but it means that you stay with something through sequences. You can do something to make that sequentiality very tight. For example, if you're doing something and I quickly said,

"What are you doing now? What do you feel in your chest? How did you say that? Where's your tongue?" If I stay with you like that, I'd get a tight sequentiality, and I'd get a buildup of tension. You can also have a loose sequentiality. If we're talking to each other, and I suddenly start telling you a story about my years in graduate school, we're going to have a loosening up of our sequentiality. Sequentiality exists whether you like it or not. What you pay attention to may have a looser or tighter quality. I deliberately—not deliberately in the sense that I strategize it—but I knowingly will go back and forth between a tight and a loose sequentiality. People don't know quite what I'm doing. I sometimes do it with surrealism, which loosens up the tightness of the sequentiality: I do it with humor. It isn't that I do it with that purpose, it's just that I noticed that it happens when I did those things. Then you come back prepared for the new experience in a new way. Then you can go to the tight sequentiality again. It's a matter of loosening and tightening. I got the tightest sequentiality from Paul Weisz. He could also go loose, from a Zen position. Fritz had a looser sequentiality, but there was always a high tension level anyway because there was magic in the air. Paul Goodman was very willing to have a very loose sequentiality and low tension. Not that what he was doing was not exciting, because for me it was. But when I would be in a workshop with him, the personal threat was not continuingly as high as it was in workshops with Fritz. So that was an important difference. But you see what Paul did was to bring through his own personal function, he brought in humanity. He was a human person, even though there was a sense of awe of his range of being. There's no less awe in my mind for Paul Goodman than for Fritz Perls, but it was a very different kind of awe. It was an awe, like, if he were an uncle, or someone in my family, how could someone in my family have that broad a range of experience? Whereas, with Fritz it was a feeling like, "I've never known a magician, and now I know what a magician can do." I never experienced Paul Goodman as a magician; I experienced him as a member of the community who just was so broad in his knowledge, so learned, and so experienced, that I was awed at how he happened to get past the family strictures. The story telling, the humanity, the curiosity, the humor, the playing around with people, the relaxedness—all of that was a part of Paul.

JW: And Laura?

EP: I had my first individual session with Laura. There was one workshop when Laura came when we were doing individual therapy as well as workshops, and I had a session with Laura. In just a very short period of time she did some things with me that were very eye-opening. As I now recognize, they were very simple things that she did, but they were very knowing. She had me be my father. I had said something *about* my father, and then I found for a moment what it was like to *be* my father. I could feel her union with me on it. I could feel her universality about it. I felt in her, as well as in the others, a grandness of experience. I thought I would be able to learn a lot from her about specific language things, specific movements. Later on when I was in a workshop with her, I saw her very finely tuned in to specific things that people were doing. She knew how to develop those things. What I noticed in her that I didn't notice in Fritz or in Paul Weisz, perhaps not in Isadore either, was a—what shall I call it?—a way of warming in to the person she was working with. She would physically move in closer to the person. She would smile. She would say encouraging things on the side. She was not afraid to be openly supportive through her gestures and movements.

JW: When I first went into training with Laura and wanted to work on something in group, there was a physical problem in terms of her location and my location and what astounded me was that she immediately got up and moved closer to me. I was astounded that I did not have to move into a "hot seat."

EP: Yes, Laura would do things like that. I was broadened by feeling that kind of personhood in her. I experienced her brightness and I also experienced her sexuality. In fact, that first session I had with her, the only private session I ever had with her, was in her hotel room. She and Fritz had come to town and they were staying in a hotel and that's where my session was. I had a feeling of her sexuality. She had never been seductive, she was just natural, she was just a naturally sensual woman, and I had never been with a woman on that kind of a professional-personal mixture basis. I felt the warmth of the sexuality and the inspiration of the professionality joined together. It just warmed my heart to be with her. That made it easier for me to do what I had to do in the session. So it helped to broaden my own experience.

Earlier in the conversation, Miriam Polster entered the room. She made herself comfortable, listened to the dialogue, and was asked to join us with . . .

JW: Miriam, at what point in time did you become involved in Gestalt?

MP: Somewhere around 1956 or so.

JW: How did you move into it?

MP: By going to groups, groups that Fritz would lead. And Laura, and Paul Goodman. I did not work with Paul Weisz. I worked with Isadore in individual therapy. And when Isadore came to town he would stay at our house. I went to graduate school in 1962. So I had a good five-six years' experience in Gestalt. And when I went into graduate school, all the other theories were new theories to me. It was almost a reversal of what happened to most people. For me the basic theory was Gestalt, and how did the other theories illuminate it?

JW: How did that make graduate school for you?

MP: A little crazy. It was a crazy experience. Because at that time there was the overt statement that psychologists didn't do therapy, just testing. I knew that it was radically different from that outside in the real world.

JW: And when did you start doing therapy?

MP: About '65.

JW: When did the Cleveland Institute begin to evolve into a formalized training program?

EP: I can't remember the year—I did practicums and lecture courses for about three years, so I would imagine that the training program must have started around '63 or so. Or '62 perhaps. But what happened after that was that we began to feel ready to teach others who were not among our group. So we announced a program.

JW: In addition to you, who were the other people from Cleveland who were teaching?

EP: We did workshops for people outside of our own community before we did our training programs. So the training program had two different directions in its evolution. The workshops were not limited to professionals. We would do workshops which would be three nights and a weekend. Dick Wallen would do the conceptual part first, and then I would do the therapy for the rest of the evening. For the first three nights. Then Fritz would come in and do a weekend. The people who taught in our first training programs were, in addition to me, Elaine Kepner, Bill Warner, Rennie Fantz, Sonia Nevis, Miriam, Ed Nevis, Joseph Zinker, and Cynthia Harris. We started out with a program of a year and a half. The training group felt it wasn't enough. They wanted to make it a three-year program. So the faculty went ahead with them and also made the next group a three-year program.

JW: And then from then on, generally speaking, the training followed that system, the three-year program?

EP: Yes. And then we introduced the intensive program. We called it intensive because it was condensed in time. You could get a full-time program over a shorter period of time. The three-year program was a weekly meeting plus a couple of workshops, plus individual therapy. The intensive program was a full-time program for a month in the summer, a week in November, a week in March, and two weeks the following summer. And that was designed for people who didn't live in Cleveland.

JW: At what point in time did the Cleveland Institute go on into areas other than Cleveland?

EP: I went to Chicago to do a group with people in Chicago. They wanted more training after that workshop. From that evolved an alternation among us on the Cleveland faculty of going to Chicago, to provide training.

JW: Is this the group that then started the Chicago Institute?

EP: Right. The next group was in Boston. I did a workshop there. And then they wanted more training. Joseph Zinker and I came in to interview the people who applied and several others of the Cleveland faculty joined us in working with them.

JW: My last historical question. Your leaving Cleveland. What was it that took you to California? What's different for you out there?

EP: It's difficult to identify exactly, but let me give you some factors that entered into our leaving. First of all, we had been talking about the city we would like to live in that we would move to—not in our retirement, but in a statement of some new way that we wanted to live. And our original talk was always about moving to New York. We almost did. I was doing a lot of things around the country already, and I was interested in writing. In fact, our book was already done by the time we moved. and we wanted a benign climate that would have visual beauty. Cleveland's winters were just too hard to bear. I had come to do a workshop at AGPA in New Orleans, around 1967 or '68 in February. When I was walking off that airplane, I said to myself, "I am not spending the rest of my life in Cleveland." It took about five or six years after that, before we finally moved. Another thing was that it's exciting to both of us to start all over again. And we chose a place, in fact, where that was most indispensable, because we knew nobody in San Diego from before our experience with San Diego. We had heard of people there. We took a trip west, we liked the people we met, and we decided on San Diego as the place we wanted to be, considering all the other warm-weather spots that might have visual beauty.

JW: And you have an institute now in San Diego?

EP: Well, we call it a training center. Basically Miriam and I do the work, and we find that it's very exciting from the standpoint of—I'm saying we again.

MP: I'll correct you if I disagree.

EP: OK. We've talked about it, so I know what Miriam feels about it. But the idea of working with people all the way is a blow-out of involvement instead of taking a section here and a section there, as we did in Cleveland. And though, as I say, I was very excited with the work in Cleveland, in either the three-year program or the intensive program, it didn't have the same feeling of following through all the way as I now have. I just love that feeling. What I miss is the kind of comradeship right in the middle of our work which I did have in Cleveland, the sense of support—

MP: And colleagual interaction.

JW: A question for both of you: People often talk of three styles of Gestalt; the West Coast style, the East Coast style, and the Cleveland style. I wonder if you're in harmony with that kind of division.

MP: The distinctions for me are hard to make, because they often boil down to the individual who's doing it. There might be some difference in the muscularity of one person or the cerebrality of another. But I'm reluctant to consider those East Coast, West Coast, Mid-West differences.

EP: Suppose you were to look at the people whose effect is most broad in the areas. . . and you look at New York, you see Isadore and Laura, obviously. But then you also see other segments of people. So you get a range right there. You would hardly say that Isadore and Laura would do the same therapy. Magda Denes I've never seen work. I've never seen the others work, either. I know something about them, but I think you'd find great differences among them. What would be the dominant difference? I don't even know. I would have more to say about the dominant quality of Cleveland and California than I would about New York. In Cleveland, I think the sequentiality is looser, in terms that I mentioned before. I think California is likely to have a tighter sequentiality. But California is mixed up for me. Because there is California, and there is also the fact that we are in California, and the people who come to us can't function in the same way as they would if they worked, let's say, with Joseph Zinker.

JW: In your book, *Gestalt Therapy Integrated*, you develop a new contact-boundary interference-deflection. I'm interested in how that came about—how that evolved in your thinking and in your work.

EP: When I was writing the outline for the first course I taught, I included deflection and expanded it later on when I did it in the book. I think that's the sequence. I just felt like it took care of some events that weren't taken into account by the other resistances that were described in *Gestalt Therapy*. There were four there. I thought of resistance in terms of direction of energy. Introjection is from out to in. Projection is the arrow going from in to out. Retroflection is like this, sort of a hairpin experience. Confluence is two individual energies going like this and meeting. And it seemed to me a lot of experiences didn't really come back like retroflection, nor did they go out, like in projection, they just missed the connection. Abstractions just don't make the mark, for example, they just vaporize in air. Or, if I don't look at you, that's deflection. The visual deflection is an important event.

MP: It may also be that it's a product of the times. I think we are in a period of increasing depersonalization. And deflection is a depersonalized way of avoiding contact. Sometimes, given all the good intentions in the world, we don't even know who the target might be for a particular feeling, for a particular point of contact. And all we have left is the deflection possibility. I buy a bicycle for my child; I see it in a store, there it stands. When I get it delivered, lo and behold, I get it, unassembled, in a box that comes like this. Now who do I get mad at for that? I go to put it together. The directions say point A and point B, and fasten it with nut Z, and so on. And point A and point B don't even meet. There I am, this experience is palpable, and *who* do I get mad at?

JW: And so the result is to deflect.

MP: Yes, I have no choice. And I have also gotten bitter. And I think as we become an increasingly urbanized population, deflection is an increasing mode.

EP: A young cousin of mine, who had been in the Army, came over to talk to me. Apparently he wanted to talk to me about some problems. I didn't know him very well, but I knew his father quite well. He's one of my closest cousins. He sat, like you're sitting there, and there's a TV set over there. And our reflection was in the TV set. And he spoke to me looking straight at the reflection in the TV set. The TV set wasn't on, just the reflection. That's deflection!

JW: Must have been interesting to experience.

EP: Yes. It may have been right then that I thought of deflection, I don't remember.

JW: In terms of the example you just gave, you had an opportunity for contact, to perhaps alter the deflection. What about in the situation Miriam mentioned, with the bike, is it just that one is left with . . .

EP: Well, of course there they've really removed the object. You have no power but to be patient, until you create the image of the bike because there is no visible bike. It's a very drastic illustration because it's as though the bike has vaporized, there are only pieces. Deflection would mostly deal with when there actually is somebody or something there that you turn away from either visually, or you turn off your hearing, or you say, "Yes, but," so that the person can't really get quite what you said. Or, if I ask you a question, I may discover after a while you've never answered my question. You've been clever enough to address the topic, but you've never answered my question. Those are all deflected things.

JW: I just thought of Ron Ziegler, Nixon's press agent . . . his frequent statement, "Yesterday's statement is inoperative."

EP: Inoperative. Beautiful deflection.

MP: George Orwell. If you want a good example, read *1984*. Double think and double speech.

EP: You know, it's interesting that you bring this question up. do you know that I've been teaching deflection for . . . well . . . the book came out in '73 . . . it took us about three years to write it . . . and I was teaching it for some years before that . . . and I think you're the first person who's ever asked me about it. I think everyone just takes it for granted that it's part of the original Gestalt system.

JW: That could support my theory that an awful lot of people doing Gestalt have not read *Gestalt Therapy*. What about dreams? A lot of people seem to think that the primary purpose of Gestalt dreamwork is to work with the disowned parts of the personality—that the dream always contains disowned parts of the personality, which is, I think, Otto Rank's original concept, not really Fritz's.

MP: Valid, yes. But exclusive, no. There are times when a dream is an attempt to come into contact with some aspect of the individual's existence. You say disowned; I think maybe it's also unavailable. It can be unavailable in that the contact they want to make with a person or an aspect of their life is, in some ways, not available to them. Or something they are perhaps just beginning to make contact with. Or making contact with at that moment, in a certain way that they haven't done before. So disowned means only that I've given it away. Unavailable means that there's a reality about it, and there are some aspects of it that have not been current in my life. It can either be an individual or even a quality of my life. Some quality of myself that I have not exactly given away, but haven't claimed. Now it's knocking on the door saying, "Pay attention to me."

EP: I have some trouble with that word, disowned, also. I would much prefer to say "not experienced." "Not appreciated." "Not recognized." Something about disowned, that possessive aspect of it . . . like when I'm actually working with a person, I would not be likely to say, "You have disowned your sexuality." I might say, "You're afraid of your sexuality."

JW: There have been teams—male/male, female/female, and male/female, who work together in Gestalt therapy, although not many. Mostly it's been things like Fritz and Laura, Fritz Perls doing Fritz Perls as a therapist, Laura Perls doing Laura Perls as a therapist. People like Ed Nevis and Sonia Nevis in Cleveland. You're recognized as a team I think mostly because of the book. Erv and Miriam Polster, working as a team, and we're here in a workshop, led by Erv and Miriam Polster, and I'm interested in hearing your comments about working together, how you work together, how you don't work together. Why you do what you do, why you don't do what you don't do.

MP: Our work together as a team is only of about five years' duration. Before that, we did only a small amount of work together.

EP: We would do an occasional workshop, couples workshops . . . that's all we did together in the old days, though we did write the book together.

MP: But our working as a team is a kind of unique way of working as a team also. Because, though we're here together, and our training in San Diego also, we divide the group into two, and each of us goes off into a room with them. So our work as a team . . . we merge for some activities, and separate for others. It's an interesting experience separating and then coming together.

EP: We're together part of the day with the whole group . . . maybe a quarter of the day . . . and then we're not together . . . the rest of the time. Also we design together. Make decisions together.

JW: We're talking now primarily about training?

EP: Yes.

JW: The part of the day that you're together . . . what happens then, and what happens the part of the day that you're apart?

MP: The part of the day that we're together is usually the didactic part of the day. When we're presenting some topic, some material.

EP: Even then we tend to alternate in our presentations.

MP: As to who is primarily responsible.

EP: Yes. There's one person primarily responsible, and the other may join in, with some things that we want to say. But may not. There are other times, of course, when we're involved in the middle of just a discussion, where there's nobody primarily responsible, but we joke around together, we tease each other some together, we don't have a lot of dialogue together . . . . .

MP: Well, no, but our ideas frequently trade off. Something that Erv will say triggers off something that I will say. Something I will say triggers off something that he will say . . . Our ideas may play off of each other's. And also, we alternate responsibility. For example, if we have a topic for presentation, and a demonstration, one of us will do one, and the other will do the other. And we alternate that way. One day Erv will do the topic and I'll do the demonstration, and the next day I'll do the topic and he'll do the demonstration.

EP: It would have been difficult for Miriam to co-lead with me in the early days. In fact, she couldn't even be a student with me. The other students at the same time were students in my practicums, in therapy with me, and such as that, and you were not in a position that we could do that. But once Miriam got on her own legs and knew her professional competence, then it was okay.

JW: How did you know?
MP: How did I know I was professionally competent?
JW: Yes.
MP: Well, I suspected I was. (laughs) And had enough independent experience.
EP: In fact, one of the great things in California is that there's no way that Miriam in California is "my wife." There are as many people who are oriented toward her offerings as mine. And it comes as an independent thing, because they know her. But in Cleveland it was different.
MP: The way I dealt with it then was to have a whole series of experiences independent of Erv and the Institute. I did a lot of teaching outside of the Institute. At that time, I didn't travel a lot; I do travel a lot more now, independently, without Erv. We do also travel a good bit together, and some without each other.
EP: We haven't done as much separately as together.
JW: One of the things I was struck with in re-reading your book in the last couple of weeks was that there was no attempt to separate the "I" in terms of the narrator.
EP: I think that's very interesting. . . because we had some quarrels about how to handle that, and finally wound up with that way.
MP: It felt so labored doing it, that we took the easy way out to get the fluidity. With the "I." There are very distinct differences, though, in the way we work.
EP: Oh, Yeah!
JW: What are the differences?
MP: Erv is crazier. When we work together, Erv is crazier than I am. I have this thing where if Erv is crazy, I feel like somebody has to not be crazy. And it's me. When I work by myself, I'm more likely to be crazy. To claim that part of me that I don't use as much when we work together.
JW: What's being crazy?
MP: What looks like irrelevant. I could describe his style of working, and he could describe mine, that might be interesting.
JW: Yes, let's do that.
MP: Erv has a kind of—Erv has a way of being very concrete—just taking experience for its own sake with the kind of simplicity that is obvious only the minute after he's commented on its obviousness. Until then it has not

been obvious. Erv is masterful at that quality of experience and at the free-association kind of leap—when you're putting together, in a way that's Sherlock Holmesian. Erv will frequently make a marvelous leap into putting something together with consistency . . . simple perceptions—that are simple only after he says it. He has this quality of perceptive simplicity. That's the way Erv works. And there's also a kind of contagious excitement—you're really interested in the person you're looking at.

JW: How do you see Miriam?

EP: She offers a very attentive staying-with a person wherever they're going. Until the special moment comes for what turns out to be a beautiful experience. There's a preparatory period, a preparation for that moment, and her experiment comes, and then through that experiment the person will take off and discover some new aspects. She's more compatible than I am, that is, the person working with her is not as likely to be afraid as with me. They trust her. And they experience what they want. She has a selectivity of language that is clarifying. And a kind of warmth that is supportive. People are freer, I think, to go in directions altogether of their own choice than they would be with me. And Miriam has a respect for the person's direction that is not clouded by her own needs, as much as mine are.

JW: About women's roles in our society. It seems to me that women have been looking lately for role models . . . and having talked and dined with some people from your group last night, it was obvious that some of the women were using you in a very positive way as a role model. I was wondering if you find that a burden, a joy, a confusion, or none of the above?

MP: All of the above. The burdensome part of it is—and this would hold true for men or women, whoever is perceived as a role model—when I'm perceived as a role model what I am as a person gets obliterated or destroyed or twisted around to fit somebody's needs as a role model. It does get burdensome.

JW: What do you do when they don't see you clearly?

MP: Talk louder. I make myself a hell of a lot clearer.

JW: Gestalt has been in existence now for roughly 25 years. What do you see happening for you in terms of the directions you'd like to move in, and what are some new things that you're excited about?

MP: One of the things that amuses me, as I think about the future, is that Gestalt therapy and Gestalt therapists have to watch out. There are dangers of respectability, which are beginning to accrue. How to remain vital although respectable is important to me.

EP: It's very hard for me to get a sense for the future, but I would like to see a few different things. One is a sense of returning to the conservative. Conservative in the sense of Gestalt therapy being captured out of the alligator mouths of the opportunistic with their quick sell, easy understood ideas about Gestalt therapy. I would like us to be less narrow in the general imagery about Gestalt therapy. The recognition of what is an abuse of the quality of exchange rather than obliterating it. For example, I would like there to be a recognition of the uses to which words like "should," "why," and so on can be put, rather than writing them out. I'd like to be able to get a broadening within Gestalt. I think there's a recognition that Gestalt therapy went too far into the manufactured language, or the manufactured non-language. That's one side of it. Another side of it points in the direction of how can Gestalt therapy carry us into the things that are interesting to people in the future? Can we, for example, be oriented with the principles of Gestalt therapy and still explore clairvoyance, extra-sensory perception . . . ?

MP: Or what Joan Fagen was fascinated by when she wrote about the fact-that some principles of Gestalt therapy may be compatible with what we're now finding out about left-brain, right-brain. That's a really intriguing possibility.

EP: Yes. That kind of thing. I think one of the problems of psychoanalysis was that they were not willing to assimilate new discoveries in such a way as to alter their system. I think our principles lead into some of the things we're talking about, in such a way as to be relevant to those. I would not have to give up what I see as very orienting to me in Gestalt therapy. I would not have to give that up in order to explore extrasensory perception. I feel like I could fit that in. Now if I couldn't then I'd have to find some other system. But I feel that for Gestalt therapy to be fully realized it has to go beyond the insights of the originators and the kind of things they had to deal with. And it's exciting to me to see whether it can encompass another generation of innovation.

JW: Some people have said that what has to happen to Gestalt is what happened to psychoanalysis. That there has to be someone like Fritz who suddenly decides to go against it.

EP: That's true at the point when that system will no longer encompass the new.
MP: Then you *must* go outside in order to make changes in direction.
EP: And it is true that psychoanalysis could not encompass what Fritz was doing. I'm not saying that it should have to. But I would be interested in seeing how far our principles, our fundamentals, stretch into the future, in encompassing the explorations of the contemporary in the future. For example, how does the concept of contact boundary become relevant to clairvoyance? Can you still use the concept of the contact boundary? I can well imagine that the concept of the contact boundary would be very relevant. It would be a new way to see it. Or a new way to sense it, perhaps. If we take clairvoyance, if we take nutrition, if we take right-brain, left-brain, if we take technology, if we take all the things that are likely to be coming in on the future . . . . .
MP: Yes, like neural transmission, the electro-chemical neurology of behavior . . .
EP: What ever those new forms are, you still have internal dialogues as relevant, experienced at a much more immediate level. So I would like to see how far into that future the Gestalt orientation would still be novel, still be fresh.
MP: I would like to see us developed enough to return to the respect for articulateness. We place great value on sensory awareness, and understanding and appreciating sensation. But I would like to see that made compatible with what we know about the Whorfian hypothesis of language. I can make just as many discriminations as I have categories. Like the Eskimos have 26 words or so for snow. I would like to see a return to the respect for language in Gestalt therapy as a tool whereby my awareness can be made more discriminating. I would like to see that rhythm restored. But I have some despair about it. I think our culture's language is getting poorer, rather than better. We're inundated with slogans. I would like to see a return to having my language being useful and workable enough so that I can make more subtle sensory discriminations. That's a direction we need to go.
EP: Another direction for the future that I have in mind is how to include within Gestalt therapy, or in any frame of therapy, the experiences of everyday life—as religion does. For example, to have some way of dealing with it not only in the therapeutic situation but in the community at large. I've had

these concerns for a long time and nothing has ever come of them because I've never been willing to change my life to explore them. But, for example, there's nothing within Gestalt therapy or within any therapy that deals communally with the time when somebody dies. Or when somebody reaches puberty. Or the daily kind of activity like prayer or mutual involvement, that goes beyond the position of specifically sought therapy. And I see some aspect, some permeation, of therapy generally into everyday life, where you would have community and rituals, and procedures and availabilities, that go beyond the old medical model that we're still dealing with. We're still afraid of the word religion. And we're still afraid of control by central authority. But the result is a kind of unavailability.

JW: As you speak of religion in daily life, I think of ritual gatherings around meals, prayers at a few specific times during the day—a way of coming back to center. Are these the kinds of things you're talking about?

EP: Yes, that's the kind of thing I'm talking about. But it's hard to talk about those things, because they feel very much like they support the wrong personal behaviors and conformities. And distortions of what life is actually about. I'm not talking about doing that, I'm talking about the kind of thing that will repeat the orientation so that one can stay tuned in. Keep it available so that one doesn't have to go to psychotherapy to relate on those levels.

JW: To the clergy instead?

EP: Oh, that's a possibility, too. The leadership makes a difference. But also people without leadership in a particular setting.

MP: It's very interesting, the association I have with that is that psychoanalysis has what they call lay analysts . . . and "lay" is also a religious term.

JW: Like lay preacher.

MP: Yes, and it may be that what you're talking about is establishing a laity, like a therapeutic laity. Or a therapeutic knowledge.

JW: Earlier, when you were describing the initial way you were working with Isadore in Cleveland—reading portions of the text and stopping when someone had a question—it occurred to me that it's a classic description of a traditional Christian bible study group.

MP: It's also a classic description of a Talmudic study group.

EP: Yes, and that was a very interesting way to be together. In fact, what I didn't say before is something along these lines. . . . when Isadore came to town he was at the center of a communal development. There was a holiday spirit.

MP: I had that with Isadore too. As frequently as he came, there was a special quality about it.

EP: So, what I see as unlikely, but valuable, is some of the Gestalt holidays. That sounds like such a trite thing to say, and I can hardly get it out of my mouth. It doesn't have to be called Gestalt holidays, but the sense of holiday, the sense of celebration, the sense of being together during times of mourning, the sense of community, is still a matter that people have to work out in their own lives, quite independently of anything to do with therapy. So if something bad happens in my life, I have to relate to the people who are part of my life, and that's okay with me. There's a certain independent spirit that comes out of that. Although I say this would be beautiful, it would be hard for me to do it. But I could do it now, I could find a way of doing it. I think it's missing in my life, even though I've replaced it with other things. But I miss the part of my life that has that in it. And the only way that I could close to that would be, for example, to go to a temple. But, what they say there is not what interests me. And the people there don't really get a chance to relate to each other, so there's no big deal about that anyway. But nevertheless, both functions are realized in the other religions, the religions other than psychotherapy. But psychotherapy has still not taken that on itself. It's still a medical model.

JW: Any last comments?

EP: I want to say something more about the Cleveland situation. There *was* a sense of community among us. There was a lot of live and let live quality.

MP: The excitement was the communal and individual discovery of talent. Learning to recognize the talent that was there. That was very exciting. Supporting it and letting it move on.

AN ORAL HISTORY OF GESTALT THERAPY PART FOUR: A CONVERSATION WITH ELLIOTT SHAPIRO

Joe Wysong

Of the small group of professionals whose weekly meetings provided the ground from which the foundations of Gestalt therapy grew and who founded The New York Institute for Gestalt Therapy, the first such institute in the world, only two reached heights that would far surpass those of their colleagues — both in fields outside the realm of psychotherapy. Those two were social critic/writer Paul Goodman and educator/psychologist Elliott Shapiro.

Shapiro is probably best known for his activities as the advocate/principal of New York City's P.S. 119 located in Harlem which continually made the front pages of New York newspapers and was chronicled in detail in writer/critic Nat Hentoff's book, Our Children Are Dying, *published in 1966. The book details the myriad of problems — ranging from the rat infestation of the school to the indifference of the central school board — facing the children, their parents, and the Harlem community where the school was located. Even more, it paints a moving portrait of a man dedicated to improving the conditions within the school (as a direct result of Shapiro's efforts, a new school building, now P.S. 92, was constructed and, interestingly enough, Paul Goodman's architect bother, Percival, was its designer) and who is also highly skilled in political maneuvering.*

Elliott Shapiro was born in the Washington Heights section of New York City in 1911. He's a big man, over six feet tall, and in his youth engaged in the typical youthful sports, with a special emphasis on boxing and fencing. The boxing was encouraged by his father and was helpful in contending with a certain amount of anti-semitism. He began working at an early age and delivered newspapers in the morning while he attended Erasmus Hall High School. He also worked in a steam laundry and a shoe factory. His father died in 1927 and when Shapiro graduated from high school he went to work at the North American Ironworks to join with his brothers and mother to help support the family.

As the depression caused business to decline sharply at the Ironworks, Shapiro was laid off and he enrolled in day courses at the Maxwell Teachers Training College in Brooklyn while working nights and weekends at a subway newsstand. Maxwell closed two years later and Shapiro enrolled for a year at the City College of New York, acquiring enough credits for a New York City teaching license. He began his teaching career as a W.P.A. remedial reading teacher at P.S. 202 in Brooklyn in 1935. In 1936, Shapiro started to teach reading in the children's ward of the Psychiatric Division at Bellevue Hospital in Manhattan. In 1937 he moved to the adolescent ward in the psychiatric division of the hospital. He remained there for eleven years.

Meanwhile, Shapiro continued his education and received a B.S. from New York University in 1937 and his Master's degree from NYU in 1946. The New York University School of Education awarded him a Ph.D. in clinical psychology in 1959.

In 1948 Shapiro became the first principal of P.S. 612 in Brooklyn. The school was located in the Psychiatric Division of Kings County Hospital and was one of the first of the New York City "600" Schools organized for children with emotional and behavior problems. He also established a day school for children who otherwise would have been sent away to other state institutions.

In 1954 Shapiro became principal of P.S. 119 in Harlem. In Hentoff's Our Children Are Dying, *Shapiro says of this appointment:*

> *I was looking for a challenging school...because I had a fairly unusual background and felt that I was qualified to deal with children who had problems. I came to Harlem, however, with some presuppositions that I found out were wrong. I had expected that children, growing up crowded together in broken*

homes, would present problems similar to those manifested in neurotic children. I have discovered that, on the whole, they do not. Most of the children here are as 'normal' as children in middle-class neighborhoods. But they do have overwhelming problems to deal with. It's to their credit that they maintain their courage as long as they do, especially when you consider that those of us who should be giving them support — teachers, school principals, and social service personnel in general — are unable to because we're so outnumbered. I found out that, for the most part, I was not working with neurotic children but with deprived children. And people like me were among those who had been depriving them. It also became clear that my work as principal had to extend into the community.

During our conversation, Shapiro and I discussed certain aspects of his work as principal of P.S. 119. After some consideration, I have deleted them from this edited version of the conversation and have limited the material included to that which relates to Shapiro's involvement with the development of Gestalt therapy. Space considerations prevent me from doing otherwise. For those interested in the details of Shapiro's career at P.S. 119, I highly recommend the Hentoff volume, Our Children Are Dying. *Excellently written, it details the problems facing the Harlem community where P.S. 119 was located and chronicles the efforts Shapiro spearheaded to contend with them.*

After his work at P.S. 119, Shapiro became the Director of the Center for Innovative Education in Rochester, New York. Although the Rochester Board of Education wanted him to remain there, strong community demand in New York City brought him back to serve as the District Superintendent for Manhattan's lower East and West sides.

While still principal of the 600 school at Kings County Hospital, Shapiro began the part-time private practice of psychotherapy in 1951. He taught at the New York Institute for Gestalt Therapy from 1952 to 1955 and again in 1959. His teaching career has included classes in psychology and education for Brooklyn College, the City College of New York, the University of California at Berkeley, and in the in-service training program of the New York City Board of Education. He also served as a Seminar Associate at Columbia University and, after his retire-

ment from the New York City School System, he became a visiting professor in the doctoral program at Yeshiva University.

In 1939 Shapiro married Florence Fishkin, a Phi Beta Kappa graduate of Hunter College and an English and Latin teacher in New York City junior and senior high schools. They have two children, a son, George, and a daughter, Ellen.

Our conversation took place on June 17th, 1985, in the living room of the Shapiros' apartment located in Manhattan's Peter Cooper Village. Florence Shapiro was an interested listener, frequently contributing the correct name, place or date when Shapiro or I floundered.

JW: What was your personal and professional background up until the time that you came into contact with Laura Perls?

ES: Well, let's see. I was head of the Board of Education Psychiatric School at Kings County Hospital in Brooklyn. I started there in 1948 and I stayed there until 1954. For twelve years before that I was at the psychiatric division of Bellevue Hospital in New York City where I taught the youngsters who came for observation for greater or shorter lengths of time. Usually for shorter lengths because many of them were court cases who were remanded to us for observation and stayed for perhaps 30 days, but sometimes for 60 days, or 90 days. But we had some youngsters who were neurotic or psychotic aside from kids who were, let's say, socially maladjusted in the sense that they were considered juvenile delinquents and so on. The neurotics and psychotics stayed for a somewhat longer time while the hospital decided what was to be done for them and what their destination was to be. Very often, of course, they were sent off to state institutions. I say "of course" because they were poor kids who, unfortunately, were not sent to private psychotherapy. I should also include the mentally retarded and borderline adolescents who were sent to special classes, institutions, or to mainstream classes with various recommendations.

Now I should say that before that I was a W.P.A. remedial reading teacher, that I worked in P. S. 202 in Brooklyn. The principal there had a great feeling that I was going to accomplish something in education. He also felt that he should become a superintendent (as he did much later) and wanted me, I think, to be very much on his side and support him. I was very much interested in organizing a teachers' union and the principal felt betrayed that here I was helping to organize the union rather than supporting him. So that when I heard that there was an opening at Bellevue I applied and moved into Bellevue in 1936 as a remedial reading teacher and worked in the children's ward with Dr. Lauretta Bender who was, I think, one of the most innovative of all the child psychiatrists in the world. Also at Bellevue at that time was the man who later became her husband, Dr. Paul Schilder, who I think Freud considered to be the person who was going to be his successor. Tragically, he was killed crossing the street. He was a very remarkable man. In fact, they named a form of Alzheimer's Disease, Schilder's Disease after Schilder. A brilliant man. Absolutely brilliant. I got to know him, and especially Dr. Bender, rather well and we met socially once or twice and had our discussions-arguments. I should mention also that David Wechsler prepared his universally used intelligence tests during this period when he headed the Psychology Department. We were quite close, but I was especially close to Florence Halperin who developed such fine insights into Rorschach testing with disturbed children.

During my student days at Maxwell Teachers College, which closed down in the middle of my undergraduate career, and later at City College, I was interested in the theory of relativity and for whatever reason, I'm not quite sure, I won the college essay prize for an article on it. But what I was really interested in was dialectics, starting with Hegalian dialectics, of course Marxian dialectics, and Engels' Anti-Duhring which I considered more valuable for me than Marx's *Capital* because of the philosophical nature of the work. And maybe influenced by Duhring, I became interested in Morgan's emergent evolution and Smut's creative evolution. Both theories stressed the importance of the whole as opposed to the part and, particularly Morgan's, how one can't predict the next complete whole — the next complete whole as an artistic verity or an artistic unity about which we've had no experience.

An example I gave very often in my own talks is that if we had never seen water boil and now here is water getting hotter and hotter and hotter and now it is 200 degrees, now 201 degrees, now 205, now 206 — even when the water has reached 210 degrees we wouldn't know that it would start to boil at 212 degrees unless we had seen it happen before. We wouldn't have been able to predict it. And I've often thought, and discussed and maybe argued a bit with people, that there are creative happenings that are in a sense unpredictable because certainly another element enters and changes the entire gestalt to such an extent that before it occurred you would not have been be able to predict it. All of this was interesting to me at the time and is related to what might be called those creative jumps in Gestalt therapy.

JW: So long before your initial contact with Laura and Frederick Perls, you were already reading much of the theoretical material that was later basic to the development of the theory of Gestalt therapy.

ES: I was always interested in Gestalt psychology because it has a theory of closure, which in a sense is that creative jump I mentioned before — that the mind makes a creative jump. When there are enough elements you suddenly see a whole that you wouldn't have been able to see before. But this isn't quite the creative jump of, let's say, a new entity. The closure jump occurs when the new element or elements allow you to infer or achieve a creative conclusion. The "emergent" jump occurs when you actually see it happen. It cannot be foretold.

So I guess I was almost ready made to fall into Gestalt therapy. But I didn't know about Gestalt therapy until a teacher at the school at Kings County, Carl Fenichel give me a copy of *Ego, Hunger and Aggression*. Carl was a wonderful teacher who later founded The League School for mentally sick children. The school is still in existence many years after his death, near Kings County, now in a separate building.

Carl had gone to see Laura and he'd come back with *Ego, Hunger and Aggression* which I had not found on my own. The book, of course, interested me very much and so I then went to see Laura, too. I think that was during my first year at Kings County — or maybe the second year. I'd had a long time feeling, a philosophical feeling, for Gestalt therapy. I had studied with Wertheimer at the New School, for instance. A wonderful man. Solomon Asch was in the class as a kind of additional authority. I don't know if you know the name now, but he was really quite a famous contributor of years back in regard to Gestalt psychology. I should note, too, that about a decade earlier, Bender had devised the famous Bender Visual Motor Gestalt Test, which I had helped edit and that Schilder had devoted many pages to Gestalt psychology in his seminal *Mind, Perception and Thought*.

Later I got my master's from N.Y.U. and quite a few years later my doctorate in clinical psychology from N.Y.U. There was almost no interest in the graduate schools in either Gestalt therapy or Gestalt psychology so I can't say that my graduate studies have contributed a great deal to my knowledge. Maybe a bit in regard to the Rorschach and various other tests: otherwise relatively little.

Somewhere along the line I should mention I was a member of the Socialist Party. Florence, my wife, was a member of the Socialist Party too. We participated in quite a few events during the Depression, including testing of civil rights against Mayor Hague in Jersey City when the Socialist Party Presidential Candidate, Norman Thomas, was beaten up. I had known he was attacked because we were there and we were all sort of attacked, but I didn't realize how badly he was beaten up until just recently when I came upon an account of the incident in a book I've been reading. And, of course, we participated in marches on Washington and that kind of thing. I think that I learned there — or maybe I even had known it before somehow — but somewhere along the line I recognized two things: 1) that people who are ambitious are on the whole cowardly on behalf of their ambitions; and 2) that it is important to develop somewhere some countervailing power if you are going to contend with the ambitious people who are at the top of the bureaucracy or who are trying to move towards the top of the bureaucracy. If you know both you can contend with them with a certain measure of success. I was also helped by the fact that Florence evidenced no worry about what I was up to.

JW: You need to create your own power?

ES: Yes, you have to find a way of creating your own power and the power that you create has to be the kind of power that will embarrass the people who are ambitious or who are in positions of some power, starting with the assistant principal, the principal, and so forth. Each one. And if you have the ability to embarrass one or the other, or whichever one that you are electing to embarrass, that person knows it. And he's is going to treat you very carefully.

I don't know what all this has to do with Gestalt therapy except that it has to do with the ability to dare, to take a chance, you see. And actually in Gestalt therapy, really what happens so often, is that in a relatively safe environment the patient is encouraged to take a chance in some area where he wouldn't have taken a chance before. So in a sense during all my struggle with the power structure, I was prepared to take a chance because I was pretty certain that no matter what the threats would be those threats would not be carried out.

JW: While all this was going on, at the same time you were involved in the formation of The New York Institute for Gestalt Therapy. How did the Institute get formed?

ES: It didn't get formed. It was like Topsy in *Uncle Tom's Cabin* — it just "growed." And, by the way, the Institute has a history of being like Topsy and that's all to the good. Everyone there was strongly sensitive to bureaucracy. It was interesting, out of all the people who were there, who had come from various places and various kinds of occupations, jobs, and had all kinds of different experiences, without exception all had the very strong feeling that a bureaucracy was a disease. It was a chronic disease of some kind. And we were clear that if anything was going to be developed in regard to this Institute, it must not be a bureaucratic Institute — one that gives degrees or gives certificates. During the early years the Institute had nobody taking care of it. Even now it has almost that same flavor. In the many years since I've retired from it, they've finally gotten somebody who at least sends messages that inform you when the next meeting is going to occur and what the topic of the meeting is.

Because of its anti-bureaucratic attitude the New York Institute has lost, as it were, in competition with the other various Gestalt institutes around the country. These other institutes, including the Polsters (whom I like), have developed formal training programs of one kind or another. The New York Institute has remained remarkably true to its original feeling that we were there together. They're still there and still acting there together. They discuss or do whatever it is, but almost never do you see an "organization."

JW: Paul Goodman, Laura Perls, Frederick Perls — they were anarchists in the most positive sense of the word.

ES: That's true — so was I, both an anarchist and a democratic socialist — which is not the contradiction that it appears to be. Another interesting fact that I mentioned in regard to Laura Perls when I said a few things at one of the meetings that was held in honor of her 75th birthday is that she's a very vital figure. She could easily have taken the lead of the institute. She has charismatic qualities of one kind or another. Even though she's been very busy with Gestalt all the time and spreads the message here, there, and everywhere she never, almost like it's an act of will, played the kind of leadership role that you would expect. One which would have developed an organization which would have become powerful, clear-cut in its statement in regard to Gestalt principles with various levels of not only membership but classes, a sort of school — the kind of thing the Polsters have done. She refrained from it. And it's to her credit that she was able to refrain from it because there's no doubt she had all the qualities to take charge. But she didn't take charge.

JW: She was, however, ever consistent in her efforts to keep the New York Institute alive and vital.

ES: Yes. She was always true to the Institute. She was always there. And when you ask her what she's doing, she says "I'm keeping my nose to the grindstone."

JW: So in those days in the beginning there was you, Paul Goodman, Paul Weisz...?

ES: The people who were there originally were Paul Weisz, Paul Goodman, Isadore From, Allison Montague, a fellow named Peter who had produced a small movie that was a very big critical success. I don't recall what the movie was about, but it was a critical success. I can't remember his last name. Then there was of course Buck Eastman, Jim Simkin, Paul Oliver, and Paul Weisz's wife Lottie.

JW: I'm surprised. In all the reading I've done, in all the conversations I've had with other early pioneers in Gestalt therapy, and even during the other interviews we've done for the *Oral History of Gestalt Therapy*, this is the first time I've ever heard Allison Montague's name. Can you tell me something about him?

ES: Allison Montague was a formally trained psychiatrist at Bellevue Psychiatric. I knew him very well during my years at Bellevue but it wasn't until the New York Institute began meeting that I discovered that he was interested in Gestalt therapy. A very tall, good looking man. Many of the women at Bellevue would eagerly have been very serious with him.

To my surprise, when I came to the group for the first time, he was there. This was the initial meeting of the group — the first time for us all. And it was startling to me that he was there because he was a psychiatrist, absolutely formally trained in psychoanalysis at N.Y.U. and had been at

Bellevue for a long time and was very highly regarded there. I was surprised to see him because I believed none of the rest of us were regarded very highly professionally anywhere. Wherever we were we were probably thought of as mavericks. I would never have thought of Montague as a maverick. Some years later he died in an accident. At the time of his death he had become the official psychiatrist at Columbia University for the students, undergraduates and graduates both. When he died, I felt it personally because I liked him very much. In our few personal contacts, here and there, we got along rather well. I think we enjoyed each other's company.

JW: The Institute met regularly at 315 Central Park West on Manhattan's Upper West Side. What kinds of things took place?

ES: Laura said, "Well, we'll have our professional group in a kind of group therapy session." Our professional group consisted of all the people I've mentioned together with Fritz, of course, and Laura. And some people I'm sure I'm leaving out.

The original group met consistently for two years. We hammered at each other, and hammered, and hammered — every week. And it was the most vigorous hammering you can imagine. I recall a friend of the assistant principal at P. S. 119, a doctor, to me a very able, very nice man, who was interested in perhaps moving into psychotherapy on a professional level. He came to one of the meetings and when he left he spoke to our mutual friend, namely the assistant principal. He said he had never witnessed the aggressive and profound battling that went on in those groups. Nobody, virtually nobody, was safe at anytime.

If you could live through these groups and take the corrections, the insults, the remarks... All these remarks were offered in some kind of professional way, in a professional sense, but with great emotion. And often, even though they were offered in a professional sense they were picked up by the recipient as being unprofessional: that this doesn't come from your professional self, this comes from you. And then that person gets hammered after having hammered somebody else, then the next person immediately gets hammered, and so on. This happened to everybody, including Fritz, who did not appreciate it, particularly when it came from Paul Goodman.

JW: Was the criticism of Fritz primarily from Goodman?

ES: No, everybody criticized Fritz, but Paul's criticism was most sustained. Paul would often say to Fritz, "The problem with you Fritz is that you're not sufficiently verbal, that you're really not an intellectual." He would say this and almost cause the conflict of sibling rivalry. He'd say, "Laura's intellectual. You're not an intellectual." That kind of thing. But Fritz would respond in kind — or unkind.

The interesting thing was that no matter how they hammered at each other at these meetings, after they were over many of us would go out and have coffee together. We'd all be in good spirits and forget that we'd been almost murdering each other.

JW: What was it that you were hammering out? Ideas? Personal feelings? Everything?

ES: I don't know that it was so much that we were hammering out ideas, really. We were doing, in a sense, psychotherapy on one another and we were picking up what we saw or heard or imagined we heard, whatever it was, and we picked it up very emphatically. Later on when I participated in or heard other group therapy sessions everything seemed so mild compared to this. Some people couldn't take it and quit finally.

I later read *The Gestalt Therapy Handbook.* I was amused to see an article by Jim Simkin who said he left New York because Paul Goodman and Elliott Shapiro were loading elephant shit on him and he didn't feel like having that much elephant shit dumped on him.

He had been working at a V.A. Hospital in New Jersey and he made, it seemed to me, rather interesting contributions to the group. Another thing the group did from time to time was to talk about what they did with their patients at a given time. Sometimes the group became a clinic conference. The patient in absentia was being described in his relationships with his therapist. And very often those relationships were being corrected by various other members of the group, especially Simkin's relationships with his patients. There was much, "Oh, you're doing this because..." directed at Simkin. It seemed to me Jim was hit pretty heavily, and again, I think, primarily by Paul Goodman. But he indicates in the article that I hit him heavily. I didn't think so. Of all the people there, I thought I was the most kindly. Anyway...

JW: A short interruption. Was Magda Denes in this group at this time?

ES: She came towards the end. That's right. I'm glad you mentioned her. She impressed us as an attractive, very bright, young person. We were all quite a bit older than she. And there's no question that she was very able. She got her doctorate relatively quickly. Those of us who were working for a living took a long time getting our doctorates. She's made a very big name for herself. As a matter of fact, I referred a patient to her recently. It's my only contact with her in the last 20 or more years.

Paul Weisz's wife, Lottie, was also there. She was also a psychiatrist at Bellevue although I didn't remember her there that clearly but I did kind of recognize her when I got to the group. Except for Fritz, the only people there who were M.D.s were Eastman, Lottie, Paul Weisz and Allison Montague. There may have been others; I don't quite remember them. I remember our talking about developing the group as a group and also as an institute. And there was always the train of thought, "Yes we ought to develop this as an institute but we have to be careful that nobody's in charge, nobody's authoritative, that we were all equals, one way or another, that we were all equals."

I think our concerns about authoritarianism and equality got in the way of the Institute in many ways, but nevertheless I respect it very highly, and I respect the fact that they've managed to keep things that way all through these years.

JW: Your activity at the Institute was before the Perls, Hefferline and Goodman book had been published?

ES: Before. Perhaps a year before.

JW: What can you tell us about its development?

ES: I spoke to Paul Goodman about the book many times. I remember very clearly saying that it was a shame that the book was published the way it was. I felt that the first part should have been the last part. Even better, I would have preferred that it not be in the book at all. It should have been a separate handbook of some kind.

I had been teaching Abnormal Psychology at Brooklyn College from 1948 to 1952 in the afternoons and evenings and had been using material from *Ego, Hunger and Aggression* in my classes. The students were working the exercises from it as a kind of term paper, reporting on experiences such as their internal listening — doing all the aspects of the exercises and reporting on them. The papers got to be rather engrossing. So, in a sense, I had done about the same thing as Hefferline had done at Columbia. It was natural to do it that way once one was a Gestalt therapist. I had collected the material but never thought really to use it. Hefferline had the creative notion to at least incorporate it into something.

Hefferline seemed kind of strange to me. He started coming to the group towards the end of these sessions. He certainly wasn't there during the first couple of years. He never contributed. He was quiet and nobody picked on him that much for being quiet either. He was almost just a piece of furniture.

JW: He was able to be quiet and get away with it.

ES: Yes. And then gradually he moved away from Gestalt therapy. He got to be interested in what might be called biokinetics or something like that.

JW: Let's go back to the writing of *Gestalt Therapy.*

ES: Oh, yes. So, I said to Paul, "This really is your book." And Paul said, "Yes, one of the problems is that Fritz is no writer (he had said this often to Fritz so he wasn't talking behind his back). He's not gifted with words," and so on. Although I realize he did write a very good paper in 1948 which was, I think, in some ways more intellectual than *Ego, Hunger and Aggression* [Shapiro is speaking here of "Theory and Technique of Personality Integration" which was later reprinted in John O. Steven's Gestalt Is in 1975]. But Paul felt very, very strongly that he had written the book. He was somewhere between hurt and embittered by the fact that he was not considered the principal author of the book.

Paul had expressed the feeling that what ended up being book two should have been book one, but it was the publisher who pushed putting the "handbook" first. The publisher believed that it was an era of self-help books in regard to psychotherapy, psychology and so on. This was a reaction, I think to the large number of sessions that would go on in psychoanalysis, that people had to spend all that money and time. So the publisher, Arthur Ceppos, believed that the first section would popularize the book. As it turned out, the first section depopularized the book for people who might have read the actual book. People felt this was something too much like a self-help book and that it didn't lend credibility to the basic theory of Gestalt therapy.

JW: It would appear, though, that Ceppos was wrong as the book did not sell well at all in the early years of its publication.

ES: No, it didn't. It did not sell well at all. I feel he was really quite wrong.

Now there are other people whom I should mention in more detail. Paul Weisz. Paul Weisz was very, very smart, quite learned. He was particularly interested in eastern philosophies. He made, it seemed to me, some of the best contributions to these sessions. He was not so bitterly attacked, either. There was the respect that one has when listening to a true intellectual. And I think that he was a fine therapist. I really believe that he, Isadore From, and Laura were probably the three best therapists. Maybe Paul Weisz was the best therapist. I felt his loss keenly. It's unfortunate he didn't write because he made what seemed to me rather important contributions. And I think he was very successful, at least much more successful than most, as a therapist.

One thing that became interesting to me at these sessions was that there often would be various dramatic events in which one of the other group members became, as it were, the center of attention in which he was asked to live through experiences that he indicated were symbolic or traumatic to him. Some experience that symbolized, let's say, a relationship to the father. And it would be worked through and the person, of course, would have an intense emotional experience there. It was a true "Ah Hah!" experience with crying, or whatever, and a sudden release. And immediately you saw a big change.

But over a period of time we realized that while these big changes might be instantaneous, they lasted for only a short period of time and that you had to continue to work at it and work at it and work at it. This was an insight that most of us developed during these sessions. What bothered me was that the West Coast people never developed this understanding. Not even Fritz ever developed it.

Fritz was a kind of salesman. First he would go off and become a salesman in Cleveland. I believe, though, that Isadore From was responsible for the lasting impression in Cleveland. Then Fritz would go off and become a salesman in Florida. He suggested that I should go to Florida. He said that he would guarantee me a thousand dollars a month there and that if I didn't make the thousand he would make up the difference. And in those days a thousand dollars a month was a lot of money. I didn't take him up on it. And maybe just as well, in the sense that he was not someone whom you relied on in regard to money. But in any case it was interesting that Fritz would be able to come back and report all kinds of successes here there and everywhere, and in a sense, I think, those successes were reported accurately, historically.

What bothered me about Fritz was that as he developed these various innovative ideas, you know, the empty chair kind of thing, and so on, he seemed to depend too much on it. And what he did was develop a kind of travelling act, especially as he began to make those short movies. And they were very impressive. I was in the audience in a number of places where these were shown. I recall one time we met at the Carnegie Endowment Center opposite the United Nations. A big hall there was filled with young people, well dressed young people who were either college or graduate students, it seemed to me, at Yale, Vassar and various places like that. It really astounded me that all these well dressed people had come. I was conscious of the fact that these were well dressed people because by this time most young people weren't well dressed. And the young woman who was at the heart of this moving presentation was present and she became a movie star whom people virtually asked for autographs and that kind of thing. I saw the weakness of it, but when I was asked to be the final discussant I made only some polite remarks. I didn't say what I wanted to say.

I realized that there was quite a difference in how I thought about Gestalt therapy. Gestalt therapy did have a kind of admonition, "You're intellectualizing." When you were in therapy yourself or with other people the statement was often made, "You're intellectualizing." And there was a verity to it. But there was, I came to believe, a twilight zone and that you might go overboard and that you might, as it were, under-intellectualize. That's what happened to the West Coast people. They under-intellectualized.

There's a difference between intellectualizing and being an intellectual. I think that's one of the things that came out of California in the 1960's and 1970's — not only that Gestalt therapy interfered with intellectualizing in terms of self-understanding, it also did not believe in being an intellectual.

After Fritz died there was a memorial service held at one of the local elementary schools and Paul Goodman gave the basic talk. In his talk Paul didn't say entirely the polite thing, for he accused Fritz of not having been an intellectual and of leading Gestalt therapy down the wrong road and that because of him Gestalt therapy was becoming anti-intellectual. Something of that nature. Similar to the things he'd said to Fritz during the early days of the Institute.

JW: Did people get angry?

ES: Oh, yes. There were people there from other cities, including some people from the West Coast. They were sitting around and they were very angry. Particularly, I think, because they weren't prepared for Goodman giving Laura the credit that had long been denied her — credit clearly due her. This was resented very much. In a way it was a talk that wasn't in the best of taste for a memorial service!

JW: During this time period that we're talking about, in addition to attending the Institute meetings, you were spending most of your time at Kings County Hospital, then as Principal of P.S. 119, plus you had a part time private practice.

ES: Plus I was also a researcher for the Jewish Labor Committee on labor reports. I reported on what might be considered brotherhood articles in the labor and minorities press and produced a 35 page paper at the end of each month. I went through about 300 minority papers and, of course, the labor papers and wrote a monthly column for these papers. I also started taking my courses towards my doctorate.

JW: What impact did your relationship with the New York Institute have on your career as an educator and political activist?

ES: Well, as things broke one way or another a lot of things happened that appeared in the press and got other media coverage and as Fritz, Laura, and the two Pauls saw all of this I felt their support, their enjoyment, and their feeling that this was a kind of extension of the daringness that they were trying to develop in therapy and, in a sense, in their own lives. After all, Fritz was daring, going all the way through America and almost the world with his maverick point of view. Laura, too, and of course Paul Goodman lived a life without boundary. Isadore From was very active in this regard.

So at that time I felt well supported by the people at the Gestalt Therapy Institute, and I knew I could see in the expression on their faces when I came in, especially when some episode had occurred, because episodes were occurring with some frequency, that they derived great pleasure from it. Finally, while I was still at P. S. 119, Paul Goodman, greatly to my surprise, dedicated a book to me — *The Utopian Essays and Practical Proposals*. I consider it a fine book that is completely ignored in a way, but some of those essays are really tremendously insightful and profound. Really remarkable essays. It's pretty hard to find peers in anybody else's writings. But not many bought the book. It finally is out again in paperback. I would say that I had that feeling of great support and when the Harlem community, the P. S. 119 home community, threw a dinner for me the Perls came, Paul Goodman came, I'm not sure who else, but we had quite a delegation from the Gestalt therapy group come to this dinner and it was very nice to see that. They had learned about it. I hadn't told them about it. I don't know how they learned about it actually, because the people in Harlem didn't know about them.

JW: I'd like to read you a statement from the book Paul Goodman co-authored with his architect brother, Percival, *Communitas* and have you react to it. "In the educational community, the mores are in principle permissive and experimental and the persons form almost invariably a spectrum of radical life from highly moralistic religious pacifists, through socialists and LaFolette or T.V.A. liberals to free thinking anarchists. The close contact of such persons, the democratic and convivial intermingling of faculty and students, leads inevitably to violent dissensions, sexual rivalries, threatened families. It is at this point that the community could become a therapeutic group and try by its travails to hammer out a new ideal for all of us in these difficult areas where obviously our modern society is in transition."

ES: There's a lot to that but there's something of Summerhill in there — too much of Summerhill in a way, because aside from what it did contribute philosophically as far as education is concerned, Summerhill did not move, as it were, in a larger society. The school has to move into the larger society and provide praxis, insights, its changes, the developments, and so on. I have a feeling that this really doesn't occur if its based that much on Summerhill. I have the feeling, the strong feeling, that first the child has to know that he lives in a world that is sufficiently secure so that he can take chances, and that he can learn this only if the grown-ups, the immediate grown-ups in his life, provide a secure world without providing a passive world or a world that allows the child to manipulate the grown-ups. A school has to provide an understanding by the children that the adults know what they're doing, that they're there sufficiently, that they're able enough, as it were, to be protective, so that they're not in danger. Since you're not in danger then you're able to experiment, to do things that you might not otherwise do.

JW: Isn't that almost identical with what you said about the therapeutic setting?

ES: That's right. That's right. I believed that for a long time, actually before I went to Gestalt therapy. I remember that I brought material that we developed at our school in the psychiatric unit of Kings County Hospital to the early meetings of the New York Institute for, basically, the two Pauls, Paul Weisz and Paul Goodman, to look over. They appreciated what we were trying to do.

Now what was interesting there was that we got into trouble in Kings County, when we developed our school there, because it got to be recognized that the school was doing things with the kids that the psychiatrists were not doing.

JW: If I remember correctly, the hospital director tried to close the school.

ES: Yes, particularly the day school. First the hospital director tried to close it. He didn't really think psychiatry was a branch of medicine, so he didn't care much for the psychiatric program in the first place. Then the director of the psychiatric unit also tried to close the school. The director, Dr. Potter, who was also a president of the American Psychiatric Association, felt that the school was being too psychiatric and was encroaching on the grounds of the psychiatrists. They were very sensitive in regard to that because by this time the Rorschach had become popular and the psychologists had been encroaching on the psychiatrist's turf with it. The psychiatrists began to feel that psychology was going to enter into the private practice of psychotherapy and — lo and behold! — our school came in and was doing a kind of group psychotherapy and achieving a great deal, I must say, in the classroom, to the extent that we were able to develop a day school. So, obviously jealous of our success and concerned that we were taking over their role, they tried to close us down. In order to develop a countervailing power, we got the New York City Committee for the Children involved. It was a very prestigious group that didn't really have a large membership, but had the wealthiest people in New York on it — one of the Rockefellers, a Gimbel, and so on. Trude Lash, the wife of writer Joseph Lash, was the chairman of the committee. Then there was Charlotte Carr who was a famous social worker. And Judge Polier, who was really a famous Family Court judge during that period.

When we were just about to be closed down, they got to the Commissioner of Hospitals of the City of New York and he overruled the directors who wanted us closed. We were to be closed down the next week so it was an overriding victory. It was received by the top doctors there in silence.

There was really a real measure of achievement. There were some youngsters who were considered hopeless. For instance, [Shapiro now points to a striking painting on the living room wall] this portrait was made by a person who was a member of the day school at that time. He was about sixteen years old. He has since become a very well known Puerto Rican painter and they're going to name a wing of the Barrio Museum on upper Fifth Avenue after him. Now, we were told absolutely conclusively by the psychiatrists that there was no hope for him. He would end his life up as a vegetable in a mental hospital. He passed away at the age of 52 after being happily married and very productive. He produced thousands of paintings. He led a real life, and here is a person who was supposed to be a vegetable in a hospital.

That's what we began to discover at the day school — that because the children were poor their prognoses were poor. And the prognoses were poor because there were tacit assumptions that the psychiatrists made and they remained tacit, for the psychiatrists never realized that they were making them. If the kids had been a little better off, they would have had different diagnoses and different prognoses and it would have been recognized that they would benefit from therapy somewhere. But because our kids were poor nobody would do anything with them and therefore they were hopeless.

We discovered that there was a big socio-economic meaning to prognoses. When we expressed this at the hospital some of the younger psychiatrists agreed with us but on the whole it was not favorably received.

JW: As you progressed in your career you became more and more distant from the children you cared about so deeply.

ES: There's something very unfortunate in this and I've thought of it from time to time. When I'd just been appointed District Superintendent another of the superintendents for whom I had some regard said to me: "Elliott, when you become a superintendent you're going to find that you're far removed from the children. And you're going to miss it very much." And it was true, I did miss it as a superintendent. I didn't miss it as a principal that much because even in the big school, P. S. 119, which at its top had sixteen or eighteen hundred kids — a horribly overcrowded school — I didn't feel distant from the children whom I knew virtually all by name. It wasn't that much of a problem with me because I really remained close. Whether it was at Kings County or at P. S. 119 or P. S. 92.

The big change occurred when I went to Rochester and was director of the Center for Innovative Education. We developed a nice group, got around the city, and developed this school. As a result of our efforts, we received a lot of federal funding, you know, that kind of thing. But I was no longer part of the entire community. I was part of the adult community. I was separated from the kids then.

And I was separated from the kids, on the whole, as a superintendent, too. Although in my first office down on the Lower East Side I was in the middle of an enclave of project houses so I could get out there in the street a bit. So they knew who I was. The kids all called me "Bignose." They'd be down the block and say, "HEY, BIGNOSE!" and I would wave to them. But, when they'd come close I'd tell them to call me *Mr.* Bignose.

But it's true, I was more separated from the kids. More slowly in my case than, I would think, in most cases because, by and large, whatever I had been operating with, as long as it was a kind of closed enclave, we were involved with the kids even though it wasn't, let's say, as a teacher in a classroom. But this is an excellent important question that raises an issue we need to explore.

JW: What do you see for the future of Gestalt therapy?

ES: I'm glad to see that at least some Gestalt therapists are beginning to think seriously that they should be going past the age of gimmicks. And there're some very good people currently involved in Gestalt therapy. That's really very important.

We're contending with the fact that the psychiatrists now have medication and are, to some degree, using it unwisely, primarily because they have a vested interest now that they are doctors of medicine again. With medication a person comes in for five minutes, gets his prescription and leaves. And the psychiatrist charges him a hundred or a hundred and fifty dollars just for giving him the prescription. The patient comes back in three months for a check-up and another prescription — for another hundred and fifty dollars. And then again. So these days the psychiatrists are moving up on the scale of economic reward and they have this vested interest in continuing to do so. So you have a whole profession, the psychiatric profession, geared not to psychotherapy anymore, but geared primarily to medical treatment of anything from mild neurosis to deep psychosis. For the psychiatrist, it is costly to do psychotherapy. Unless he's doing psychotherapy with a very rich person and can charge a lot.

As a result, Gestalt therapy, like all the other therapies from the other psychological schools, has to contend with the growing pressure to rely on pills. I think the pressure will continue to grow. Psychologists, therefore, have a redoubled responsibility for psychotherapy.

I'm especially interested in the ability of Gestalt therapy to get the existential message of psychotherapy out to the public. Existentialism by now is forgotten, if not unpopular. I still believe very much in what might be called the existential philosophy. I believe that there are Gestalt therapists who seem to believe in it, who in their own professional work try to extend it.

JW: You just mentioned that existentialism is now forgotten. Would you expand on that?

ES: Well, existentialism as an idea was really extremely popular in the 1960's. Not that many people knew what existentialism was, but people talked about existentialism. I tried that out in a number of classes, including a class that I taught in Berkeley one summer. I had a hundred and eight people there and I asked them to define existentialism. First I asked them how many of them had heard about it. Oh, well, they'd all heard. I then asked them to define it. Nobody could define it.

I think Gestalt therapy offers the ability to develop individuals who accept their powers, their talents, their abilities, and then to use these talents and abilities to allow them to experiment. As a matter of fact, one doesn't know one's talents and one's abilities unless one experiments with them. Because then you develop new creations of one kind or another. New art forms. New gestalts, let's say. That jump, as it were, from one stage to another. I think that there are people who are Gestalt therapists who are successful in helping to develop individuals who *practice*. Because the word *practice* is the important word, in the sense that one *practices* what he believes in. If there were more time for the world, there would be more and more people who could be involved in developing something that the world needs very much. And that is the development of the individual talent of each citizen into whatever is the gestalt of the social comedy at any given time. In a sense the people who participate in a successful therapy will be people who would make somewhat larger contributions. And even if it weren't successful to the whole world, the majority of the world or even more than a small piece of the world here and there and everywhere, that would be very useful and very nice and would be an asset and would help civilization make some progress.

JW: You just said, "If there were more time for the world."

ES: That's right. I have to realize that we all won't exist that long. I have argued for a long time that we're virtually all the same age in the sense that you don't count age from birthday, you count it from "death day," as it were. And it saddens me relative to my grandchild, my grand nieces, my children, and for the other people too, generally speaking. But I don't tell them about it. I mean, what's the use?

I really threw up my hands with the atomic bomb. As soon as it came out, I saw that at some point or other it could not be controlled, and it could not be controlled because gradually these things would have to be made in secret. And there would be so much secrecy, so much depending on secrecy that people who had no business — not that anybody has business having the atomic bomb — but people who especially have no business having atomic bombs will have them. Today they're not atomic bombs, now it's hydrogen bombs. We're absolutely unable to control the hydrogen bomb. That, I think, means we're at the end of civilization.

So I have spent my time reading a lot and thinking about it, trying to figure out some way that we could develop a non-bureaucratic — a funny word in this context — a non-bureaucratic way of controlling that hydrogen bomb. I haven't been able to come up with anything. In other words, I'm sorely depressed but nobody knows it. My wife knows it, but I smile as I say it, you know, that kind of thing. And I threw up my hands, because I felt, in a sense, what am I doing this for? I don't believe there's hope for humanity. So I said, "Well, I'll address myself to the lack of hope with humanity and see if I can find some way out of this." And the situation is so far that it looks like an impossibility.

I read interminably about the various disarmament plans, nuclear weapons ideas, United States versus Soviet Russia and what can be done. And my feeling is that as bad as we are in the United States, the secret society that is Russia is the great menace, the first great menace. Secrecy is disaster making. But I have no answer for that either. I think it's quite possible that in the proliferation we will have any number of menaces pretty soon. Real serious menaces. I think we have some sign of it in the terrorist activities. A few terrorists, first of all only two terrorists, were able to hamstring the United States, Israel and the rest of the civilized world in the episode now going on in regard to the airline.[The interview took place during the third day of captivity of the 29 Americans who were hijacked and held in Beruit before their eventual release two weeks later.] Just two terrorists. Now I have a feeling that there you have symbolically what will happen. A country like Libya will be able to terrorize the world — or a country like Pakistan, may do it. They are developing, obviously, neutronium and plutonium bombs. But I don't want to go on. I don't want to depress everybody in the world.

I don't talk...you know, as I'm talking to you now... It's rare for me to do this. Some of my close friends, those I have left, know this is my point of view, but I don't talk about it much. I'm still interested in what the Mets do, the Yanks do. I follow the football games. I read and I forget very quickly now too.

I was once invited to talk at a meeting of the New York Institute for Gestalt Therapy and I went into this topic in some detail. I don't know how they happened to invite me. I guess it must have been some anniversary and I was the guest speaker. They had quite a crowd there and I came up with this statement that I had composed much more formally and in greater detail than I've done this afternoon with you. There was also a psychologist of some renown at the meeting. So I went into this topic in great detail — and succeeded in depressing everyone except the famous psychologist who came over and shook my hand with great fervor — he agreed with my position. Having depressed the New York Institute group to such an extent, they never invited me back again!

JW: That's a wonderful story. Thank you very much.

ES: It has been a real pleasure.

Made in the USA
Monee, IL
05 November 2026

67379767R10059